# MOZART
## Seen Through 50 Masterpieces

**PAUL ROUSSEL**

# MOZART
## Seen Through 50 Masterpieces

**HABITEX BOOKS**

Cover design: ANDRÉ DURANCEAU

Interior design: DONALD MORENCY

• English language translation and production supervision by:
AMPERSAND PUBLISHING SERVICES INC., Toronto

Ⓐ 2

Exclusive Distributor:
Collier-Macmillan Canada Ltd.
539 Collier-Macmillan Drive
Cambridge, Ontario N1R 5W9
Tel. (416) 449-7115 / (519) 621-2440


ISBN-0-88912-028-5


Bibliothèque nationale du Québec
Dépôt légal — 1er trimestre 1976

# Table of Contents

# Acknowledgements

I wish to express my sincere thanks to Macmillan and Company Limited, London, England, and to the Executors of the late Miss Emily Anderson for their kind permission to use her text *The Letters of Mozart and His Family* (Second Edition), for the letters reproduced in part or in whole in this book.

My thanks are also due to the Canala Council for making it possible for me to visit London, Vienna, and Salzburg. During this trip I consulted Mozart's personal thematic catalogue as well as many other important manuscripts. I must also thank the Librarians at the British Museum in London, Dr. Franz Grasberger of the Austrian National Library, and Dr. Mittringer of the Society of the Friends of Music, both in Vienna.

The illustrations are reproduced with the kind permission of the Mozarteum in Salzburg, the British Museum in London, and the Musikbibliothek Peters in Leipzig.

P.R.

*« There's nothing
better in art
than Mozart's best. »*
G. B. Shaw.

# 1

## 1777

# Concerto for piano and orchestra in E Flat Major, No. 9, K. 271

1. **Allegro**
2. **Andantino in C Minor**
3. **Rondo: presto; menuetto: cantabile**

On January 27th, 1777, Wolfgang Amadeus Mozart celebrated his twenty-first birthday with his father, mother and sister in Salzburg, the city of his birth. At that point in time, Mozart was on the verge of becoming a bitter young man.

For the previous six years he had held the post of *Konzertmeister* in the orchestra of the Prince-Archbishop Hieronymus von Colloredo and it irked him to be cut off from the two greatest centres of music in Europe — Vienna and Paris.

His office weighed the more heavily upon him because

from the age of six he had enjoyed the glory of being the most astounding infant prodigy of his day. With his elder sister Maria Anna (known as Nannerl within the family) he had been dragged across Europe by Leopold and Anna Maria Mozart to be shown off and applauded in Germany, France, England and Holland.

This frail, excitable and emotional child had been required to cope with the strain of continual travel and exhausting public appearances.

Subsequently, he made three successive trips to Italy with his father. At a time when music had to be Italian to be accepted, this young German boy of thirteen managed to win the favour of the most demanding of publics with his Italian operas.

In Rome, Pope Clement XIV awarded him the Order of the Golden Spur, six months before the first performance in Milan of his opera 'Mitridate, Re di Ponto'. Bologna welcomed him into the ranks of its Philharmonic Society. Verona honoured him with the title of *maestro di capella.* Despite such honours, when he sought a position in Vienna at the age of seventeen with the Empress Maria Theresa, he had no success whatever.

Two years later, on March 7th, 1775, after directing his opera 'La Finta Giardiniera' in Munich, Mozart returned to Salzburg, where he was fated to remain until September 1777. For a musician who had known glory during his childhood travels, these two years of reclusion were to prove unbearable.

Between April and December 1775 he wrote five magnificent violin concertos which expressed his personality in brilliant fashion. These were probably composed for his own use only, since playing the violin was one of his duties as *Konzertmeister*.

By the beginning of 1777, Mozart felt as if he were slowly suffocating in Salzburg. He who longed to write operas, was reduced to composing short, impersonal masses for a master who slighted him, and fashionable pieces for the nobles and the wealthy bourgeoisie of the city.

The people of Salzburg recognized his talent, but they could not contribute to his artistic development, nor could they help him to realize his fondest aspirations.

The young composer was well aware of the literary revolution which had been sparked in Germany by the works of Lessing and Goethe. 1774 had marked the publication of Goethe's "The Sufferings of young Werther" and 1777 was to be the year of Klinger's "Sturm und Drang" which was soon to give its name to a movement displaying, together with a certain restlessness, an entirely new style of expression and sensibility.

Mozart was all the more impatient to leave Salzburg since he knew that in his present surrounding he would never be able to produce works in the new and learned style of Joseph Haydn, a composer whom he admired and regarded as a master. The revelation of Haydn's six Quartets, Opus 20, published in Vienna in 1772, with four of the finales employing the fugal technique, had bowled him over. For it was not to be the reforms

17

of Gluck that Mozart was going to respond to, nor to the ideals of the "Sturm und Drang" movement, but to the innovations of Haydn, before turning toward Bach and Handel.

If he was ever to establish a style of his own and invent his own musical language, the first essential was to get away from Salzburg. Accordingly, he conferred secretly with his father in January 1777, and together they worked out a tour through Germany, after which both of them were to visit Paris.

While this was going on, Mlle. Jeunehomme, a celebrated pianist, arrived in Salzburg. Little is known of her except that she was a Parisienne and that in Juanary 1771 Mozart dedicated his Concerto in E Flat Major, K. 271 to her.

The following year, when Mozart was in Paris with his mother, he offered this work to the engraver Sieber, who turned it down — doubtless intimidated by its revolutionary character and its great technical difficulty.

Slowly, Mozart came to realize that the piano concerto was the music-form through which he could most adequately express the intimate personal aspect of his genius and show himself to be the greatest pianist of his day.

It was while he composed the Jeunehomme Concerto that Mozart found the exact manner by which to express intimate feelings in the form of purely entertaining music. His later concertos might be more polished, but they would never be more original.

The four concertos for harpsichord written in 1767

(K. 37, K. 39, K. 40 and K. 41) are nothing more than arrangements in the concerto style of various French sonata movements.

Mozart's first true piano concerto is the Concerto in D Major, K. 175, written in Salzburg in 1773, which has been listed as No. 5. Mozart thought sufficiently highly of it to play it again in Vienna nine years later.

On that occasion he replaced the original finale, which he considered too polyphonic, with a sprightlier rondo (K. 382) more in keeping with the taste of the times. Nevertheless, the Jeunehomme Concerto is the first of his piano concertos which is undeniably Mozartian.

* * *

**1. Allegro**  Like all concertos of this period, this one opens with an orchestral prelude. But there is one difference. Here the piano takes part in the statement of the first theme. Mozart intended this somewhat offhand departure from tradition merely as a little joke to surprise and amuse the listener. Even though the leading role is allotted to the piano, the orchestra asserts its independence in forceful fashion and with sparkling resonance, despite the fact that the instrumentation is reduced to two oboes, two horns and the strings.

**2. Andantino in C Minor**  This is the first slow movement in a minor key to appear in one of Mozart's piano concertos. It is a poetic and meditative piece, somewhat in the style of a breathless recitative, with Mozart whispering secrets to us of an almost heart-rending tenderness.

19

**3. Rondo: presto; menuetto: cantabile**   The dazzling sprightly rondo is interrupted by a peaceful and charming minuet with four variations. This procedure, which is most unusual in a rondo, had previously been used by Mozart in his violin concertos. After the minuet, we return to the rondo and to the mood of somewhat excitable gaiety that characterizes this finale.

Concerto for piano and orchestra in
E Flat Major, No. 9, K. 271

**Works written between January 1777 and May 1778**

Divertimento in B Flat Major, K. 287
Divertimento in F Major, K. 288
Aria for soprano 'Ah, lo previdi' K. 272
Mass in B Flat Major, K. 275
Offertory 'Alma Dei Creatoris', K. 277
Gradual 'Sancta Maria', K. 273
Piano Sonata in C Major. K. 309
Arietta "Oiseaux, si tous les ans", K. 307
Piano Sonata in D Major, K. 311
Quartet for flute and strings in D. Major, K. 285
Flute Concerto in G. Major, No. 1, K. 313
Flute (oboe) Concerto in D Major, No. 2, K. 314
Sonatas for piano and violin:
    — in G Major, K. 301
    — in E Flat Major, K. 302
    — in C Major, K. 303
    — in A Major, K. 305
Aria for tenor 'Se al labbro mio', K. 295
Arietta "Dans un bois solitaire", K. 308
Sonata for piano and violin in C Major, K. 296
Sinfonia concertante (wind instruments) in E Flat Major,
K. 297b
Concerto for flute and harp in C Major, K. 299
Piano Variations, "Je suis Lindor", K. 354

# 1778 | 2 Sonata for violin and piano in E Minor, K. 304

1. Allegro
2. Tempo di minuetto

On March 14th, 1777, Leopold Mozart sent Hieronymus von Colloredo a request for leave for himself and his son. His request went unanswered.

He submitted a second petition in June, but the Archbishop of Salzburg objected on the grounds that he required the services of all his musicians to entertain the Emperor Joseph II, who he expected to pay a visit to Salzburg in the near future on his way back from France, where he had been to see his sister, Marie-Antoinette.

A third request, made in July, met with a categorical refusal.

The Prince-Archbishop's hostile attitude showed only too clearly what little value he placed on his *Konzertmeister's* exceptional gifts and growing reputation. But Mozart was a proud young man and he intended to show his sovereign

*Aloysia Weber as Zemira in*
*Grétry's opera 'Azor and Zemira'.*

that he was more than simply another musician, among many others employed in a small German principality.

On August 1st, he sent a letter of resignation to "His Grace, Most Worthy Prince of the Holy Roman Empire", Archbishop of Salzburg. On this document, Colloredo scrawled in pencil: "Ex decreto Celsissimi Principis, 28 Augusti 1777. To the Court Chamberlain with my decision that in the name of the Gospel, father and son have my permission to seek their fortunes elsewhere."

In the end, Leopold Mozart was prevented from accompanying his son, since Colloredo was magnanimous enough to let him retain his post as violinist and composer at the court of Salzburg, but he felt that at 21 the boy was not yet ready to travel about Europe on his own and arranged for his wife to replace him as chaperone.

On September 23rd, 1777, Anna Maria and Wolfgang Mozart set out for Munich. Having failed to obtain employment with the Prince-Elector Maximilian III, the young composer took his mother on to Mannheim. But here, too, he was unsuccessful.

It was late October when they reached Mannheim and Mozart soon made many friends, among them Christian Cannabich, conductor of the Mannheim orchestra. At this time his was the best orchestra in Germany and also the most complete from an instrumental point of view since it contained clarinets (instruments of which Mozart was particularly fond). Mozart described the orchestra to his father as follows:

"On either side there are ten or eleven violins, four

violas, two oboes, two flutes and two clarinets, two horns, four violoncellos, four bassoons and four double basses, also trumpets and drums. They can produce fine music..."

Mozart also met Fridolin Weber at Mannheim. Weber was a copyist and prompter at the Mannheim theatre and an uncle of Carl Maria von Weber, who would later write 'Der Freischütz'.

Young Mozart also met Frau Weber, her five daughters, and her son. The two eldest daughters, Josepha and Aloysia, were accomplished singers, especially Aloysia, who was barely sixteen. Before long, Mozart fell violently in love with her.

He hardly even noticed Constanze Weber, a little girl of fourteen — his future wife.

In his letters to his father, Mozart spoke only of Aloysia, saying how wonderfully she sang in a pure beautiful voice. All she needed was some stage experience to be the lead singer in any theatre. She could read music excellently, and was even able to play his most difficult piano sonatas at sight, albeit slowly.

The young man dreamt of taking her to Italy, where he could write operas for her. Naturally, they would pass through Salzburg and, of course, he would introduce her to his father and to Nannerl. In preparation for the trip, he spent many hours with her, helping her rehearse some bravura arias.

Leopold Mozart was distressed by his son's lack of success in Munich and Mannheim and he was even more disturbed by the news of his son's infatuation for Fräulein Weber.

No good could come of that. He sent instructions for his wife and son to leave for Paris immediately.

Mozart complied obediently, although with much regret. On leaving Mannheim, he took with him Aloysia's vows of fidelity and two pairs of mittens she had knitted for him. There was also a present from Herr Weber, the comedies of Molière, with the following inscription on the flyleaf: "Ricevi, amico, le opere del Molière in segno di gratitudine, e qualche volta ricordati di me." Mozart was particularly impressed by one play, 'Don Juan, or The Stone Banquet', in which the author stresses how terrible it is to be a "grand seigneur méchant homme".

The trip to Paris took nine-and-a-half days, with Mozart forever going back over how sad he was to have left his friends in Mannheim, especially his dear Aloysia whom he had promised to rejoin as soon as possible.

Mozart and his mother reached Paris on March 23rd, 1778, only to find the city a source of extremely bitter disappointments. As an infant prodigy, Mozart had been extolled to the skies in Paris. But there was nothing particularly startling about the young man of that day: he was merely another awkward young German, murdering the French language. Nobody remembered him.

Mozart was deeply wounded by this change of attitude. He wrote to his father on May 1st:

". . . Paris is greatly changed; the French are not nearly so polite as they were fifteen years ago; their manners now border on rudeness and they are detestably self-centered. . . . You say I ought to pay a good many calls in order to make new acquaintances and revive the old ones. That, however, is out of the question. The distances are too great for walking — or the roads too muddy — for really the mud in Paris is beyond all description. To take a carriage — means that you have the honour of spending four to five livres a day, and all for nothing. People pay plenty of compliments, it is true, but there it ends. They arrange for me to come on such a day. I play and hear them exclaim: 'Oh, c'est un prodige, c'est inconcevable, c'est étonnant', and then it is — Adieu."

There were more disappointments in store for Mozart, however. Jean Le Gros, Director of the well-known Concert Spirituel, commissioned him to compose a "symphonie concertante" which Mozart completed and handed in but it disappeared as if by magic, and was never found. Mozart strongly suspected that *maestro* Cambini was at the bottom of this affair, but he was never able to prove it. "As it is (so far as music is concerned)," he complained to his father, "I am surrounded by mere brute beasts."

He made several proposals for operas but these came to nothing. He was, however, compelled to write a ballet, 'Les Petits Riens', based on what he described as "wretched old French airs". He was offered a post as organist at Versailles but it was so poorly paid he felt he had no option but to turn it down. He was depressed and unhappy. Despite having his mother at his side, he felt himself abandoned by the whole world.

"I am tolerably well, thank God, but I often wonder whether life is worth living — I am neither hot nor cold

— and don't find much pleasure in anything''.

His mother's letters to Salzburg kept harping on how she missed the joys of family life. But young Mozart thought only of Aloysia, whom he had left behind in Mannheim. He was burning to see her again, and he almost made himself ill worrying whether she would still want him when he returned to fetch her.

Such was Mozart's state of mind in May 1778, when he wrote one of the most melancholy of all his works, the Sonata in two movements for violin and piano in E Minor, K. 304. This work forms part of a group of six sonatas for violin and piano dedicated to the Princess-Electress of Munich, published in Paris in 1778 as 'Opus 1' — the second of Mozart's works to be so described. He had, in fact, already published two sonatas for harpsichord and violin described as 'Opus 1'. They were published in Paris in 1774 and dedicated to Madame Victoire, the daughter of Louis XV.

\* \* \*

**1. Allegro**  When Mozart uses a minor key, it is often an indication that he is about to make a statement of some special character. Such is the case in this *Allegro* which strikes a plaintive note from the unison introduction of the first theme. The atmosphere is tense, even disturbing. Neat contrapuntal play compresses the already dense texture of the thematic material. Twice there is a passionate outburst of violence, which then subsides. The entire movement is extremely concise in structure and marked throughout by a bitter sadness.

**2. Tempo di minuetto** Though less dramatic than the opening *allegro,* this movement continues the melancholy mood. The trio in E Major is one of considerable beauty. All charm and tenderness, it anticipates some of Schubert's Viennese waltzes. The calm interlude is of short duration. Inexorably, the minuet repeats its poignant song. The whole movement is admirable for its brevity. (Mozart is highly skilled in the art of falling silent when he has nothing more to say, a quality displayed by very few of his successors.)

The work immediately following this Sonta in E Minor, the Piano Sonata in A Minor, K. 310, is equally melancholy, but it displays less discretion and restraint. Storm and tempest reign from the beginning of the first movement, and the entire sonata is charged with emotions almost excessive in their intensity.

**Works written between May 1778
and the Autumn of 1779**

*Piano Sonata in A Minor, K. 310*
*Sonata for violin and piano in D Major, K. 306*
*'Les Petits Riens', K. 299b*
*Gavotte for orchestra, K. 300*
*Symphony in D Major, No. 31, K. 297 ('Paris')*
*Piano Sonata in C Major, K. 330*
*Piano Sonata in A Major, K. 331*
*Piano Variations on 'Ah, vous dirais-je maman', K. 265*
*Piano Variations on 'La Belle Française', K. 353*
*Piano Sonata in F Major, K. 332*
*Piano Variations on 'Lison dormait', K. 264*
*Piano Sonata in B Flat Major, K. 333*
*Aria for soprano 'Popoli di Tessaglia', K. 316*
*Sonata for violin and piano in B Flat Major, K. 378*
*Concerto for two pianos in E Flat Major, K. 365*
*Mass in C Major, K. 317 ('Coronation')*
*Symphony in G Major, No. 32, K. 318*
*'Thamos', K. 345*
*'Regina Coeli', K. 276*
*'Vesperae de Dominica', K. 321*
*Symphony in B Flat Major, No. 33, K. 319*
*Serenade in D Major, K. 320 ('Posthorn')*
*Divertimento in D Major, K. 334*

*Anna Maria Mozart. Portrait in oils
by an unknown artist.  About 1775.*

# 3
## 1779 | Sinfonia concertante for violin and viola in E Flat Major, K. 364

1. **Allegro maestoso**
2. **Andante in C Minor**
3. **Presto**

On or about June 15th, 1778, Mozart's mother fell suddenly ill. Because she had no faith in French medicine, she refused to see a doctor. Her condition seemed to improve for a few days and on June 18th, the festival of Corpus Christi, Mozart was able to attend Le Gros' Concert Spirituel and enjoy the success of his symphony in D Major, K. 297.

"I was so happy," wrote the young composer to his father, "that as soon as the symphony was over, I went off to

33

the Palais Royal, where I had a large ice, said the Rosary as I had vowed to do — and went home — . . "

On the 19th, his mother was forced to her bed, suffering from a severe intestinal infection. Mozart insisted that his mother take an antispasmodic powder for her fever, but it had no effect. He become terribly distressed and despite the protest of the sick woman, he persuaded his friend, François Heina, to fetch a doctor. The physician prescribed powdered rhubarb for his patient. However, her condition got so much worse that on June 29th the doctor advised Mozart to send for a priest. Mozart clutched desperately at his mother's hand, talking to her and weeping.

On July 3rd, Anna Maria fell into a coma. She died at ten o'clock that evening.

Mozart wrote to his father immediately, but to prepare him for the shock he told him only that his mother was seriously ill. Then he wrote to the Abbé Bullinger, a family friend in Salzburg:

"Mourn with me, my friend! This has been the saddest day of my life — I am writing this at two o'clock in the morning. I have to tell you that my mother, my dear mother, is no more! God has called her to Himself. It was His will to take her, that I saw clearly — so I resigned myself to His will. He gave her to me, so he was able to take her away from me. Only think of all my anxiety the fears and sorrows I have had to endure for the last fortnight. She was quite unconscious at the time of her death — her life flickered out like a candle . . . No one was present but myself, Herr Heina (a kind friend whom my father knows) and the nurse ... By the mercy of God I have borne it all with fortitude and composure ... I beg you, therefore, most beloved friend, watch over my father for me and try to give him courage so that, when he hears the worst, he may not take it too hardly. I commend my sister to you also with all my heart. Go to them both at once, I implore you but do not tell them yet that she is dead — just prepare them for it."

The death of his mother in a foreign land was a terrible ordeal for Mozart. However, given his excitable and active temperament and his realistic outlook, he was not the man to spend much time bewailing his unhappy lot.

No one came to weep over the mortal remains of his mother. She was buried the day after her death, and on July 9th Mozart wrote to his father.

"You will easily conceive what I have had to bear — what courage and fortitude I have needed to endure calmly as things grew gradually and steadily worse ... I have indeed suffered and wept enough — but what did it avail? So I have tried to console myself: and please do so too, my dear father, my dear sister! Weep, weep, as you cannot fail to, but take comfort at last. Remember that Almighty God willed it thus — and how can we rebel against Him? Let us rather pray to him, and thank Him for His goodness, for she died a happy death."

In August, 1778, Leopold Mozart decided to recall his son to Salzburg. It seemed pointless for Wolfgang to stay in Paris any longer. He had been away long enough. In the preceding twelve months nothing had gone well for him. He had fallen afoul of Colloredo. He had no success in Munich, Mannheim and Paris. And in Paris he had suffered the worst misfortune of all, the death of his mother. Leopold pestered his son with letter after letter ordering him to return to Salzburg and to resume his former position.

Despite his unwillingness, Mozart complied with his father's order, but he played the truant and lingered on the way, spending a month in Strasbourg where he gave a concert. Then, instead of proceeding straight to Salzburg, he headed for Mannheim, assuming that a spell in the cordial atmosphere of that friendly city would restore his spirits.

When he arrived, he learned that Aloysia Weber had joined the German opera in Munich and that the whole Weber family had moved to that city. In December, Mozart decided to go there himself to rejoin his young beloved.

He presented himself before Aloysia dressed in mourning for his mother in the French style — wearing a red coat with black buttons. He discovered that Aloysia's feelings toward him had completely changed and she seemed anxious to forget that not so long ago she had wept at his departure.

Mozart felt bitterly deceived, but rather than give way to tears, he sat down at the piano and improvised a saucy little tune, to the words: "J'emmerde qui se fiche de moi et la la la!" Later, when Mozart spoke of Aloysia Weber, he was inclined to say she was merely a hypocritical, mischievous flirt. But he had loved her and she had made him suffer.

He rejoined his family in mid-January 1779, downcast and heavy-hearted. The celebration of his twenty-third birthday, on the 27th, left him joyless.

Mozart was not given the promotion he had hoped for on his return to Salzburg. Instead of being appointed Precentor, he had to resume his post of *Konzertmeister,* to which the duties of Court organist were added shortly thereafter.

The year 1779 was rich in magnificent works: the Concerto for two pianos in E Flat Major, the 'Coronation' Mass, the 'Posthorn' Serenade, the Divertimento in D Major, K. 334, and, above all, the Sinfonia concertante for violin and viola in E Flat Major, K. 364.

Because he was such a brilliant pianist, it is easy to forget that Mozart was also an excellent performer on both the violin and the viola. In his Sinfonia concertante, he brings together, for the first and only time, these two instruments which, after the piano, he loved most.

The orchestra consists of two oboes, two horns and strings in which the violas are divided (that is, they play two separate parts).

**1. Allegro maestoso**   This movement is one of enormous proportions — expressive, colourful, and vibrant with passion. The violin and the viola converse with much warmth and animation. One makes a statement; the other picks it up, strengthens it then rounds it off. As in a human conversation, the exchange of ideas is punctuated

37

by intervals of silence.

**2. Andante in C Minor**   Here, the dialogue becomes more intimate and serious. Mozart displays consummate art in the way he shows off both the sparkling tone of the violin and the richer depth of the viola. At the end of the movement one is left with the feeling that this beautiful and pathetic love-duet could have gone on indefinitely.

**3. Presto**   This movement is a comedy full of dizzying gaiety. There is no logic to it inasmuch as the expected always turns up, but never quite the way one expected it. Surprise follows surprise in this imaginative and varied finale. The cadenzas Mozart wrote for this Sinfonia concertante are models of clarity and conciseness.

**Works written between the Autumn of 1779 and November 23rd, 1781**

*Mass in C Major, K. 337*
*Sonata da chiesa in C Major, K. 336*
*Vesperae solemnes de confessore, K. 339*
*Symphony in C Major, No. 34, K. 338*

## Sinfonia concertante for violin and viola in E Flat Major, K. 364

'Zaide', K. 344
Lieder
  'An die Hoffnung', K. 390
  'An die Einsamkeit', K. 391
  'Verdankt sei es dem Glanz', K. 392
  'Die Zufriedenheit', K. 349
  'Komm, liebe Zither', K. 351
'Idomeneo, Re di Creta', K. 366
Ballet music for 'Idomeneo', K. 367
Aria for soprano 'Ma, che vi fece', K. 368
Quartet for oboe, violin, viola and violoncello in F Major, K. 370
Aria for soprano 'Misera, dove son!', K. 369
Serenade in B Flat Major, K. 361
Rondo for horn and orchestra in B Flat Major, K. 371
Allegro of a Sonata for piano and violin in B Flat Major, K. 372
Rondo for violin and orchestra in C Major, K. 373
Aria for soprano 'Ah questo seno deh Vieni', K. 374
Sonatas for violin and piano:
  — in F Major, K. 376
  — in F  Major, K. 377
  — in E Flat Major, K. 380
  — in G Major, K. 379
Variations for piano and violin on 'La Bergère Célimène', K. 359
Variations for piano and violin on 'Hélas, j'ai perdu mon amant', K. 360
Variations for piano, on a theme by Grétry, K. 352
Serenade in E Flat Major, K. 375

*The Mozart family. Oil painting by Johann della Croce, 1780-81. The portrait on the wall is that of Anna Maria Mozart.*

# 1781 | 4 Sonata for two pianos in D Major, K. 448

1. **Allegro con spirito**
2. **Andante in G Major**
3. **Allegro molto**

Mozart was no sooner back in Salzburg than mistrust reigned again between him and Colloredo. Before long, the young composer had but one objective — to shake off his unbearable yoke and recover his independence. The lot of German musicians, tied in servitude to suffocating little courts was too humiliating for Mozart to tolerate any longer.

He was convinced that it was absolutely impossible for a musician to make a living in Germany. He himself had tried, not in Vienna, since he was a German, but in Munich and especially in Mannheim, only to fail miserably at every turn. (At the house of his friend Cannabich, he had actually been reduced to sobbing when he learned that Karl Theodor, the Prince-Elector of the Palatinate, would have nothing to do with him.)

One had to go into exile to make a career, he reasoned.

41

Johann Sebastian Bach was virtually unknown in Europe because he had never left his own country, while others had achieved fame by leaving Germany. Bach's own son, Johann Christian, and Handel, for example, achieved great success in London; Gluck, Schobert and Gossec in Paris; Hasse in Milan; and even Dittersdorf in Vienna.

Very well then, he would leave Germany.

At the end of the summer of 1780, Mozart was commissioned by Karl Theodor, then Prince-Elector of Bavaria, to write an *opera seria* for the next Munich Carnival. (It was for the Munich Carnival that he composed 'La Finta Giardiniera, five years earlier in 1775.) The new opera, 'Idomeneo, Re di Creta', was inspired by an early 18th century French tragedy. The libretto was entrusted to the Abbé Varesco, the Court chaplain at Salzburg, which pleased Mozart immensely because it meant that he would be able to work closely with the librettist.

*Opera seria* was an outdated, solemn and pompous music-form and was not very favourably regarded by up-to-date composers such as Mozart. However, he was so happy to be writing for the theatre once again, that he threw himself into his task with great enthusiasm.

At the time, Salzburg had no regular theatre for opera. Companies would, on occasion, give special performances as, for example, Emmanuel Schikaneder's troup in September 1780. Mozart wrote several songs for him and the two men quickly became good friends. (Schikaneder was later to become the librettist for 'The Magic Flute'.) On November 5th, 1780, Mozart left, unaccompanied, for

*Hieronymus von Colloredo, Prince-Archbishop
of Salzburg. Oil painting by König.*

Munich to meet the singers, direct rehearsals and put the finishing touches to 'Idomeneo'.

Colloredo also left Salzburg around this time to attend the funeral of Maria Theresa in Vienna. Under the circumstances, Leopold Mozart and Nannerl felt quite at liberty to leave for Munich immediately, to join Mozart.

The dress rehearsal of 'Idomeneo' was held on January 27th, 1781, the composer's twenty-fifth birthday. The opera opened the next day under Mozart's own direction. 'Idomeneo' was received most enthusiastically by the Munich public. Much encouraged by this success, Mozart became more determined than ever to escape from his present servitude. After the tiring business of producing his opera, the young *maestro* was glad to have the opportunity to enjoy the carnival in the company of his father and sister.

Just as he was preparing to return to Salzburg, Mozart received an order from Colloredo to join him in Vienna without delay. Leopold and his daughter consequently had to return home alone.

Mozart arrived at the Imperial capital on March 16th, and before long was involved in a series of events which precipitated the final break between himself and his master.

Mozart purposely arrived late at Prince Galitsin's house one evening to avoid being presented to the host at the same time as the other musicians from Salzburg. He was greeted personally by the Prince. Colloredo was furious at this bit of impertinence and in retaliation forbade Mozart to take part in a charity concert being given for the benefit of the widows and orphans of Viennese musicians.

Mozart countered immediately and persuaded several of his more important acquaintances to intervene with the Prince-Archbishop on his behalf with the result that Colloredo, under pressure and much annoyed, found himself with little option but to lift his restriction.

The concert in question, at which Mozart himself scored a great personal success, was given on April 3rd and featured an orchestra and chorus consisting of 180 musicians. Shortly thereafter, Mozart was involved in several violent scenes with Colloredo. During one of them the Archbishop of Salzburg so far forgot himself as to call his *Konzertmeister* a scoundrel and a rake.

Mozart wrote to his father on May 9th and described the episode as follows: "My patience has been so long tried that at last it has given out. I am no longer so unfortunate as to be in Salzburg service. Today is a happy day for me. Just listen . . . (he) called me a scoundrel, a rascal, a vagabond. Oh, I really cannot tell you all he said. At last my blood began to boil, I could no longer contain myself and I said, 'So Your Grace is not satisfied with me?' 'What, you dare to threaten me — you scoundrel? There is the door! Look out, for I will have nothing more to do with such a miserable wretch.' At last I said: 'Nor I with you!' 'Well, be off!' . . ."

Beside himself with anger, Mozart sent his official letter of resignation to Count Karl Arco, Colloredo's High Steward, that same day. Count Arco refused to forward the letter to the Prince-Archbishop and Mozart heard nothing from him for a whole month.

"The Archbishop runs me down to everyone here", he wrote to his father, "and has not the sense to see that such a proceeding does him no credit; for I am more highly respected in Vienna than he is. He is only known as a presumptuous, conceited ecclesiastic, who despises everyone here, whereas I am considered a very amiable person." Finally Mozart sent Count Arco a note asking for an interview. On June 9th he wrote to his father, giving his account of what transpired at this meeting.

"Well, Count Arco has made a nice mess of things! So that is the way to persuade people and to attract them! To refuse petitions from innate stupidity, not to say a word to your master from lack of courage and love of toadyism, to keep a fellow dangling about for four weeks, and finally, when he is obliged to present the petition in person, instead of *at least* granting him admittance, to throw him out of the room and give him a kick on his behind — that is the Count, who, according to your last letter, has my interest so much at heart— . . . ."

And so, Count Karl Arco takes his place in history as the man who kicked Wolfgang Amadeus Mozart on the backside.

Mozart swore vengeance and thought about nothing else for weeks. But vengeance was not very easy to arrange in the 18th century, especially against a high ranking member of the nobility. Little by little his anger melted away in the intoxicating happiness of his new-found — and costly — freedom. He decided to have his music and his clothes sent from Salzburg, and to settle down temporarily, or so he thought, in Vienna. In actual fact, he

*Constanze Mozart. Portrait in oils by*
*Josef Lange, Mozart's brother-in-law.*
*1782*

was to spend the rest of his life there. After his quarrel with Colloredo, Mozart left the German house where the Archbishop and his entourage were living and rented a room from Frau Cäcilie Weber, Aloysia's mother (who had been recently widowed) in a house called 'The Eye of God'.

This time, he fell in love with Aloysia's sister Constanze, who was now eighteen.

He wrote to his father in December, announcing his engagement.

"But who is the object of my love? Do not be horrified again, I entreat you. Surely not one of the Webers? Yes, one of the Webers — but not Josefa, nor Sophie, but Constanze, the middle one".

Then the young lover described his future wife, 'the middle one', in these terms: "She is not ugly, but at the same time far from beautiful. Her whole beauty consists in two little black eyes and a pretty figure. She has no wit, but she has enough common sense to enable her to fulfil her duties as a wife and mother ... Moreover, she understands house-keeping and has the kindest heart in the world. I love her and she loves me with all her heart. Tell me whether I could wish myself a better wife?"

Rumours got back to Salzburg about Mozart's being in 'The Eye of God,' and the fine time he was having surrounded by the Widow Weber and her daugthers. Leopold was angry and ordered his son to give up his room there. He advised him to move in immediately with some friends in Vienna, the Aurnhammers, whose daughter Josepha happened to be a pupil of Mozart's at that time. The master described his pupil in these terms:

"If a painter wanted to portray the devil to the life, he would have to choose her face. She is as fat as a farm-wench, perspires so that you feel inclined to vomit, and goes about so scantily clad that really you can read as plain as print: *'Pray, do look here.'* True there is enough to see, in fact, quite enough to strike one blind but — one is thoroughly well punished for the rest of the day if one is unlucky enough to let one's eyes wander in that direction — tartar is the only remedy! So loathsome, dirty and horrible! Faugh, the devil!"

Neverthless, Mozart was delighted with the girl's musical talent, and he had to admit she played beautifuly. Indeed, it was for Josepha Aurnhammer and himself that Mozart wrote the Sonata for two pianos in D Major. The work was performed for the first time on November 23rd, 1781 at the Aurnhammer home. The manuscript bears the date 1784 because Mozart made a fresh copy of this work when he played it again in June, 1784, at Döbling with another of his pupils, Barbara Ployer.

Mozart had not previously written anything for two pianos. Since Fräulein Aurnhammer was an outstanding partner for him, he decided that the work should be brilliant, ornamental and in the 'galant' style.

**1. Allegro con spirito** The movement opens with one of those sonorous demands for attention which occur so frequently in Mozart's 'galant' compositions. The dialogue between the two pianos is no less eloquent than that between the violin and the viola in the Sinfonia concertante in E Flat Major, but it is much shallower, despite certain canonic passages.

**2. Andante in G Major**   The atmosphere here is one of poetic elegance. The charming melodies heard throughout this movement are deceptively fluent.

**3. Allegro molto**   In order to let his pupil show off her technique, Mozart ended his sonata with a bravura in which she could match her brilliance with his own. It is an amusing little burlesque à la Turque, bubbling over with gaiety, much in the spirit of the would-be Turkish music which would soon be heard in 'The Abduction from the Seraglio.'

**Works written between November 23rd, 1781 and July 16th, 1782**

*Rondo for piano and orchestra in D Major, K. 382*
*Aria for soprano 'Nehmt meinen Dank', K. 383*
*5 Fugues by J.S. Bach transcribed for string quartet, K. 405*
*4 Preludes for string trio, intended for fugues by J.S. Bach, K. 404a*
*Prelude and Fugue for piano in C Major, K. 394*
*Fantasia for piano in D Minor, K. 397*

# 5

## 1781-1782 | 'Die Entführung aus dem Serail' K. 384 ('The abduction from the seraglio')

Up to the time of his break with Colloredo and his setting-up in Vienna in 1781, Mozart was financially dependent on his father and the Prince-Archbishop of Salzburg. But now, for the first time in his life, he was suddenly faced with the necessity of earning a living on his own. To fill in time until he could begin giving concerts, he took on three pupils: Countess Zichy, Countess de Rumbeke and Therese von Trattner.

Mozart's first concert in Vienna, his first major success in the capital, was given on May 26th, in the Augarten. The Archduke Maximilian and the Countess Thun attended, as well as Baron Gottfried van Swieten, whom Mozart had recently met and of whom he would see a great deal in the future.

Mozart also made the acquaintance of Gottlieb Stephanie, known as Stephanie the Younger, who was stage-manager at the German Opera. Naturally, the two men soon talked about opera and Mozart told him that, at the age of twelve, he had written a *singspiel* (a German operetta) for Dr. Anton Mesmer of Vienna, entitled 'Bastien und Bastienne'. This was a German translation of 'Les Amours de Bastien et Bastienne' by Mme. Favart, a work largely inspired by Jean-Jacques Rousseau's 'Le Devin du village'.

Mozart showed Stephanie the music he had written at Salzburg the year before for another *singspiel*: 'Zaide or the Seraglio'. Fired with enthusiasm, Stephanie proposed an entirely new libretto titled 'Belmonte und Konstanze, oder Die Entführung'. Mozart could hardly believe his own good fortune, for at that very moment what he wanted more than anything else to do was to write something in the Turkish style, which always went down particularly well with the Viennese. In those days authors' rights were non-existent and to put the plot together, Stephanie quite ruthlessly ransacked the work 'Belmont und Konstanze' from a certain Christoph Friedrich Bretzner. Bretzner protested forcefully in a Leipzig paper against 'a Viennese called Mozart' who had shamefully plagiarized his work. But that was as far as the matter went for Bretzner, the purported author of 'Belmont und Konstanze' had, himself, stolen his ideas indiscriminately from others.

On July 31st, Stephanie delivered the libretto for 'The Abduction from the Seraglio' to Mozart. Three days later, three arias were already written. The first act was completed on August 22nd, but the second act took until May

*Programme from the first production of*
*'The Abduction from the Seraglio'.*

8th of the following year, and the third until May 29th, 1782.

'The Abduction' was intended to be produced in mid-September 1781, but the numerous revisions insisted upon by Mozart (which all but caused a rupture in his relations with his librettist) and certain powerful conspiracies directed against the *singspiel,* put the opening back until July 1782.

At that time, Italian opera held sway in Vienna and naturally there were many musicians who dreaded the appearance of Mozart's new German opera, especially in view of the excellent reports about it that were being circulated. Finally, on July 16th, 1782, the first performance of 'The Abduction from the Seraglio' was staged at the Burgtheater. It was a resounding success.

In a letter to his father dated July 20th, Mozart wrote:

"I hope that you received safely my last letter informing you of the good reception of my opera. It was given yesterday for the second time. Can you really believe it, but yesterday there was an even stronger cabal against it than on the first evening! The whole first act was accompanied by hissing. But indeed they could not prevent the loud shouts of 'bravo' during the arias. . . . In the second act both duets were repeated as on the first night, and in addition Belmonte's rondo 'Wenn der Freude Tränen fliessen'. The theatre was almost more crowded than on the first night and on the preceding day no reserved seats were to be had, either in the stalls or in the third circle, and not a single box. My opera has brought in 1200 gulden in the two days."

On the 27th, Mozart again wrote:

"My opera was given yesterday for the third time in honour of all the Nannerls and won the greatest applause; and again, in spite of the frightful heat, the theatre was packed. . . . I may say that people are absolutely infatuated with this opera. Indeed it does one good to win such approbation."

For a time, it seemed that in Viennese musical circles the only topic of conversation was "The Abduction from the Seraglio" and its great originality. However, many music-lovers found the opera too complicated and especially difficult to sing. It was even said that the Emperor Joseph II, while assuring Mozart of his admiration for the work, complained that it contained too many notes, to which Mozart retorted, "Not one note too many, Sire!"

Some of the traditional criticism levelled against this opera argue: the role of Osmin is given exaggerated weight, while Pasha Selim's role is merely a speaking part; the abduction scene is not sung; some of the arias are too long; and the final vaudeville is too light.

Whether these criticisms are justified or not, 'The Abduction from the Seraglio' remains a work of irresistible vitality and warmth. It displays qualities of exhuberance and youthful freshness which Mozart would never find again. With the exception of Pamina's 'Ach, ich fühl's' in 'The Magic Flute', this *singspiel* contains two of the most beautiful love songs ever written by Mozart: Belmonte's 'O wie ängstlich' and Constanze's 'Traurigkeit'.

At the time he wrote 'The Abduction from the Seraglio',

Mozart was much more than an "experienced" composer or an artist who had known solitude and suffering. He was also a man in love, fully capable of understanding and expressing the deepest inner feeling of the human heart.

\* \* \*

In a letter written on September 26th, 1781, Mozart gave his father a long description of the first act of 'The Abduction from the Seraglio':

"I have sent you only fourteen bars of the overture, which is very short with alternate fortes and pianos, the Turkish music always coming in at the fortes. The overture modulates through different keys; and I doubt whether anyone, even if his previous night has been a sleepless one, could go to sleep over it."

*No. 1: Belmonte's aria 'Hier soll ich dich denn sehen'* "As the original text began with a monologue, I asked Herr Stephanie to make a little arietta out of it. . . ."

The song picks up, in C Major, the theme in C Minor from the *andante* which forms the middle section of the overture.

*No. 2: Osmin's lied 'Wer ein Liebchen hat gefunden', followed by a duet by Belmonte and Osmin* ". . . and then to put in a duet instead of making the two chatter together after Osmin's short song."

Osmin's short song is a *lied* in couplets, in the German style; the comic duet is a real little jewel of *opera buffa*.

*No. 3: Osmin's aria 'Solche hergelaufne Laffen'* "Osmin's rage is rendered comical by the use of the Turkish music.

But as Osmin's rage gradually increases, there comes (just when the area seems to be at an end) the allegro assai, which is in a totally different tempo and in a different key; this is bound to be very effective. For just as a man in such a towering rage oversteps all the bounds of order, moderation and propriety and completely forgets himself, so must the music too forget itself. But since passions, whether violent or not, must never be expressed to the point of exciting disgust, and as music, even in the most terrible situations, must never offend the ear, but must please the listener, or in other words must never cease to be *music,* so I have not chosen a key remote from F (in which the aria is written) but one related to it — not the nearest, D minor, but the more remote A minor."

*No. 4: Belmonte's aria 'O wie ängstlich, o wie feurig'* "Let me now turn to Belmonte's aria in A major, 'O wie ängstlich, o wie feurig'. Would you like to know how I have expressed it — and even indicated his throbbing heart? By the two violins playing octaves. This is the favourite aria of all those who have heard it, and it is mine also. I wrote it expressly to suit Adamberger's voice. You feel the trembling — the faltering — you see how his throbbing breast begins to swell; this I have expressed by a crescendo. You hear the whispering and the sighing — which I have indicated by the first violins with mutes and a flute playing in unison."

*No. 5: Janissary chorus 'Singt dem grossen Bassa Lieder'* "The Janissary chorus is, as such, all that can be desired, that is, short, lively and written to please the Viennese."

*No. 6: Constanze's aria 'Ach, ich liebte, war so glücklich'*
"I have sacrificed Constanze's aria a little to the flexible
throat of Mlle Cavalieri, 'Trennung war mein banges Los
und nun schwimmt mein Aug' in Tränen.' I have tried to
express her feelings, as far as an Italian bravura aria will
allow it. I have changed the 'Hui' to 'schnell' so it now
runs thus — 'Doch wie schnell schwand meine Freude'.
I really don't know what our German poets are thinking
of. Even if they do not understand the theatre, or at all
events operas, yet they should not make their characters
talk as if they were addressing a herd of swine. Hui,
sow!"

*No. 7: Trio — Osmin, Belmonte, Pedrillo — 'Marsch!*
*Troll euch fort!'* "Now for the trio at the close of Act
I. . . . It opens quite abruptly — and because the words
lend themselves to it, I have made it a fairly respectable
piece of real three-part writing. Then the major key
begins at once pianissimo — it must go very quickly —
and wind up with a great deal of noise, which is always
appropriate at the end of an act. The more noise the
better, and the shorter the better, so that the audience
may not have time to cool down with their applause."

In his letter of September 26th, 1781, Mozart explained
that the reason he was unable to make better progress
with the composition of the opera had to do with the
revisions he had asked Stephanie to make in the libretto.
His own descriptions of the various numbers from 'The
Abduction from the Seraglio' pretty well end here, except
for one subsequent reference to the quartet, 'Endlich
scheint die Hoffnungssonne (No. 16), with which the second

act closes in the final version. Mozart spoke of it at the time as, "a charming quintet or rather finale" opening the third act, but he said he would prefer to see it at the end of Act II. In the end, the quintet became a quartet and was moved to the end of the second act.

'The Abduction from the Seraglio' is not an opera of ensembles, as Mozart's subsequent dramatic works were to be. Indeed, this *singspiel* comprises fourteen arias for seven ensembles: one chorus; three duets; the trio ending the first act; the quartet at the end of Act II; and the vaudeville (a quintet) at the end of Act III. The Janissary chorus (No. 5) is repeated after this vaudeville and brings the opera to a close.

Constanze's great aria, 'Martern aller Arten' (No. 11) is noteworthy in that Mozart precedes it by a long instrumental prelude which includes several elements which reappear during the aria itself. This dramatic bravura scene requires the soprano to display a vocal prowess no less astonishing than that of the Queen of the Night.

In his letter of September 26th, 1781, Mozart describes Belmonte's aria 'Wenn der Freude Tränen fliessen' (No. 15) as 'a rondo'. The rhythmic accompaniment here recalls that of the romanze in the Serenade 'Eine Kleine Nachtmusik'. Continual shifts between the major and the minor keys produce a pecular effect in the charming serenade, 'Im Mohrenland' (No. 18) which Pedrillo sings in the third act while accompanying himself on the mandolin.

The duet between Pedrillo and Osmin, 'Vivat Bacchus!

Bacchus lebe!' (No. 14), is a model of brevity (unlike other pieces in the opera which are far too long). Here again, Mozart gives a 'Turkish' colour to his music by the lavish use of triangle, kettledrum and cymbals.

The duet between Osmin and Blonde, 'Ich gehe, doch rate ich dir' (No. 9), during the course of which the listener learns that the girl is 'an Englishwoman born to freedom' is equally light and charming. In contrast, the long recitative and duet between Belmonte and Constanze, 'Welch ein Geschick! O Qual der Seele!' (No. 20) seems strangely dramatic in a scene which leads to the final vaudeville.

# 1782

## 6
## Serenade for wind instruments in C Minor, K. 388

1. **Allegro**
2. **Andante in E Flat Major**
3. **Menuetto in canone in C Minor; trio in canone al rovescio in C Major**
4. **Allegro**

Four days after the opening night of 'The Abduction from the Seraglio' Mozart wrote to his father:

"Well, I am up to the eyes in work, for by Sunday week I have to arrange my opera for wind-instruments. If I don't, someone will anticipate me and secure the profits."

Mozart managed to get the arrangement for the wind-instruments done in time, but a publisher from Augsburg finished the piano-vocal score before him.

"You have no idea how difficult it is to arrange a work of this kind for wind-instruments, so that it suits these instruments and yet loses none of its effect."

When Mozart heard from his father, on top of everything else, that Sigmund Haffner was to be made a nobleman in Salzburg, and had commissioned a symphony from him (Mozart) to celebrate the occasion, Mozart felt it was almost more than he could cope with.

". . . Well, I must just spend the night over it, for that is the only way . . ."

On the following Saturday, July 27th, Mozart sent his father news of the symphony:

"You will be surprised and disappointed to find that this contains only the first Allegro, but it has been quite impossible to do more for you, for I had to compose in a great hurry a serenade, but only for wind-instruments (otherwise I could have used it for you too)."

Three days later, he made further excuses for not having completed the symphony.

"You see that my intentions are good — only what one cannot do one cannot!" Then he added a sentence which sums the man up perfectly: "I am really unable to scribble off inferior stuff".

The music for Haffner, which was halfway between a symphony and a serenade, became the Symphony in D Major, No. 35, K. 385. The following year, when it was performed in Vienna, Mozart discarded the opening march and the first of the two minuets it originally contained.

As for the serenade he "had to compose in a great hurry", it emerged as the heart-rending Serenade in C Minor for two oboes, two clarinets, two horns and two bassoons, K. 388. Its originality stems from its being written in four movements only, from its key which is unusual for a serenade and, above all, from the polyphonic effects stressed throughout the composition.

There is a question as to why Mozart wrote this tragic work so soon after the success of 'The Abduction from the Sereglio'. When he wrote his father: "I have *had* to compose a serenade . . .", was he alluding to some urgent commission or do these words mean, rather, that new and important ideas had come flooding into his mind and that he felt compelled to take the time to put them down on paper, despite the pressure of his other work?

Since his arrival in Vienna, Mozart had been exposed to a considerable amount of music by Bach and Handel at the house of Baron van Swieten, who was a great lover of polyphonic music. What Mozart heard there probably caused him to doubt some of the validity of his own work for, quite suddenly, during the spring of 1782, he started writing fugues. He transcribed five fugues by Johann Sebastian Bach as string quartets. He composed a further four preludes for string trio, intended to precede a fugue by Wilhelm Friedemann Bach and three others by Johann Sebastian Bach. Finally, he sketched out several fugues for piano in succession, but then abandoned them.

It was during this period of aesthetic crisis that Mozart wrote his Serenade in C Minor, a composition crammed with contrapuntal passages, and one of the most agitated and deeply pessimistic of all his works.

There can also be no doubt that Mozart was considerably disheartened by his father's absence from Vienna when

'The Abduction from the Seraglio' was first performed, because his letter of July 31st to Leopold is full of reproach. "I received today your letter of the 26th, but a cold, indifferent letter, such as I could never have expected in reply to my news of the good reception of my opera."

Mozart reproached his father bitterly for showing so little interest in his son's opera, which had been such a sensation in Vienna, that "...people refuse to hear anything else, so that the theatre is always packed." He added, "It was given yesterday for the fourth time and is to be repeated on Friday. But you — have not had the time."

No doubt the reason Leopold decided not to attend the première of 'The Abduction' had in part to do with his quarrel with Wolfgang over the latter's forthcoming marriage. Mozart was very distressed by this rift between his father and himself. It was a continuing source of unhappiness to him that he had to beg for his father's consent to the match in every one of his many letters to Salzburg.

On Saturday, August 3, 1782, the bethrothed couple signed their marriage contract, two days before the arrival of Leopold's paternal blessing which he finally deigned to bestow upon them. It arrived too late; on the previous day, Sunday, August 4th, Mozart and Constanze were married in a very simple ceremony attended only by their closest friends in St. Stephen Cathedral. Baroness Martha Elisabeth von Waldstädten, a good friend, gave a dinner in the young couple's honour that same evening.

\* \* \*

**1. Allegro** All eight instruments in unison state a rising sombre and mournful theme. The plaintive voices of the oboes and the clarinets seem to sing a song of profound grief. The entire movement is punctuated by passionate outbreaks of almost uncontrolled violence.

**2. Andante in E Flat Major** Despite its key, which is usually one of Mozart's happiest, this movement, at one time solemn, at another tender, continues the mood of sadness set by the opening allegro.

**3. Minuet in canon; trio in canon cancrizans** Here, Mozart shows off his contrapuntal skill. This is the bravura movement of the serenade, remarkable for its irresistible rhythmic pulse. However, it manifests a sort of nervous exasperation and its rigid style gives it an air of severity.

**4. Allegro** The finale is set out in the form of variations. The first four are in C Minor. In the fifth, in E Flat Major, the horns attempt to dissipate the stifling mood of gloom by their flourishes. The work comes to an end on a note of reserved happiness.

**Works written after the Serenade K. 388,**
**up to December 31st, 1782**

*Symphony in D Major, No. 35, K. 385 ('Haffner')*
*3 Marches for orchestra, K. 408*

*Sonatas for piano and violin:*
  — *in C Major, K. 403*
  — *in A Major, K. 402*
  — *in C Major, K. 404*
*Fantasia for piano in C Minor, K. 396*
*Aria for soprano 'In te spero', K. 440*
*Quintet for horn and strings in E Flat Major, K. 407*
*Horn Concerto in D Major, No. 1, K 412*
*Concerto for piano and orchestra in A Major, No. 12, K. 414*
*Rondo for piano and orchestra in A Major, K. 386*
*Piano Concerto in F Major, No. 11, K. 413*
*Piano Concerto in C Major, No. 13, K. 415*

# 7

## 1782 | String Quartet in G Major, K. 387 (Haydn No. 1)

1. Allegro vivace assai
2. Minuet; trio in G Minor
3. Andante cantabile in C Major
4. Molto allegro

Two days after his marriage, Mozart had the good fortune to attend a performance of 'The Abduction from the Seraglio' performed at the special request of Gluck. The famous composer showered his young colleague with praise and was kind enough to invite him to dinner the following day.

It was summer and Mozart's pupils had left Vienna. He and his wife lived happy days in their first accomodation in Vienna, an apartment in the beautiful Grosshaupt House, on the Hohe Brücke, near St. Stephen Cathedral. Four months later, the young couple moved to the Herberstein House, a few doors further along the Hohe Brücke. Such was to be the pattern during the nine years of their married lives until Mozart's death. They

*The Emperor Joseph II.*

would move a good ten or eleven times, depending on whether Mozart's star was ascending or on the wane.

Mozart felt he should go to Salzburg in the near future to introduce Constanze to his father and his sister. He was still keenly aware of his falling-out with the prince-Archbishop, so the idea of a forthcoming trip was hardly an entirely pleasant prospect.

Despite the happiness that his marriage and his first Viennese success brought him, Mozart was dissatisfied with his present situation and he was worried about the future. On August 17th, he wrote to his father: "The Viennese gentry, and in particular the Emperor, must not imagine that I am on this earth solely for the sake of Vienna. There is no monarch in the world whom I should be more glad to serve than the Emperor, but I refuse to beg for any post. I believe that I am capable of doing credit to any court. If Germany, my beloved fatherland, of which, as you know, I am proud, will not accept me, then in God's name let France or England become the richer by another talented German, to the disgrace of the German nation. You know well that it is the Germans who have always excelled in almost all the arts. But where did they make their fortune and their reputation? Certainly not in Germany! Take even the case of Gluck. Has Germany made him the great man he is? Alas no! Countess Thun, Count Zichy, the Baron van Swieten, even Prince Kaunitz, are all very much displeased with the Emperor, because he does not value men of talent more, and allows them to leave his dominions. Kaunitz said the other day to the Archduke Maximilien, when the conversation turned on myself, that *'such people only come into the world once in a hundred years and must not be driven out of Germany, particularly when we are fortunate enough to have them in the capital'."* \*

That summer, Mozart so seriously considered establishing himself elsewhere as to start taking French and English lessons. Leopold was disturbed by his son's plans and he wrote to Baroness Waldstädten, asking her to urge Wolfgang to have a little patience. It was at this juncture that Mozart began working on his Mass in C Minor, K. 427.

During their engagement, Constanze had been seriously ill and the young composer had vowed to write a mass of thanksgiving for her recovery. He worked at it throughout the summer, dreaming all the while of buying one of those fine, red frock-coats that were all the rage that season. He knew exactly what buttons he wanted on it, mother-of-pearl with yellow stones in the centre, like the ones he had seen one day at Brandau's, in the Kohlmarkt.

In October, Mozart directed a performance of 'The Abduction from the Seraglio' staged in honour of the Grand

---

\* At this time, Vienna was the capital of the German Empire and it should be noted that Mozart refers to himself in this letter as 'German'. In the 18th Century, Salzburg was an Archbishopric and an independent Principality, but Bavarian in origin. It was much closer to Munich than to Vienna. In none of Mozart's many letters is there any mention of his having Austrian status, although there are frequent references to his German nationality. It was only after the Treaty of Vienna in 1814 that Salzburg lost its independence and finally became part of the Austrian Empire.

Duke Paul of Russia. His pupils had returned from their summer holidays in the country and the concert season began again. Fräulein Aurnhammer gave one on November 3rd, and she took care to have her master take part.

On December 31st, Mozart finished a new composition, not his Mass in C Minor, but the String Quartet in G Major, K. 387, the first of his six quartets dedicated to Joseph Haydn. It was while he was involved in the composition of this quartet that Mozart resolved the problems of style which had been bothering him for the past year, and succeeded in integrating polyphony into the 'galant' music of the day.

The six Haydn Quartets mark one of the peaks of Mozart's productive career. They were written between December 31st, 1782 and January 4th, 1785, and published by Artaria (who paid Mozart a good price for them) with a dedication to Haydn in Italian. They represent one of the most troublesome undertakings of Mozart's entire artistic life. The original manuscripts are covered with erasures and corrections.

The influence of Joseph Haydn on Mozart's symphonies, and especially on his string quartets, is obvious. Mozart was far too intelligent not to recognize the importance of the older man's Sun Quartets and Russian Quartets. The impressions they made on him were among the most vivid of his career. However, Mozart never imitated them, his personality being already too firmly developed to be subjugated, even by a master like Haydn.

Two more different personalities could hardy be imagined

than those of these two men. The contrast is invariably drawn between Haydn's soothing diatonics and Mozart's often disturbing chromatic effects. On the one hand, Haydn is pleasant, calm and crystal clear; on the other, Mozart is gloomy, excitable and complex. Haydn is capable of expressing joy, pure and simple; Mozart's gaiety is always tinged with sadness. Nonetheless, the two musicians thought highly of each other. Their friendship did not become really close, however, until after the birth of Mozart's second son, Karl Thomas in September 1784. At that time Haydn paid a lengthy visit to Vienna, where he stayed in a house owned by his master, Prince Nicholas Esterhazy. During his stay, he often invited Mozart to come and visit.

When the two friends joined each other to play quartet music, Haydn played first violin, Karl Ditters von Dittersdorf played second violin, Mozart played the viola and the composer, Johann Baptist Wanhal, was the violoncellist.

The Haydn Quartets enable Mozart to establish his mastery in this particular genre. They are striking examples of a refined art-form and of an inner comprehension unmatched elsewhere in his works. The first three are the most learned and the most tormented of the series. The last three are more radiant and certainly more relaxed.

**1. Allegro vivace assai** Without preamble, Mozart expounds a theme which is triumphal in pace and generous in its breadth of conception. It sets the entire movement afire. This splendid statement is followed by a second subject which is more graceful, but no less vigorous. A little rhythmic phrase of charming cast concludes the exposition of the thematic material. This is a truly joyful movement, although the mood darkens temporarily during its development.

**2. Minuet; trio in G Minor** It was from Haydn that Mozart borrowed the idea of putting the minuet in second place. Abrupt contrasts between *piano* and *forte* give it an irregular gait. The trio begins with a frankly aggressive theme, stated by the four instruments in unison. Following this it develops into a sweet, sad song.

**3. Andante cantabile in C Major** This *andante*, a dreamy, meditative piece in which intelligence and sensitivity are interwoven, is by no means free from passion. At times it even flares up to the point of violence.

**4. Molto allegro** In this brilliant finale, the serious and the humorous are constantly at war. Mozart's unique preoccupation consists of starting on their way some fugues which are relentlessly dispelled by gay and insolent ritornellos. He begins two of them (the first one bearing a resemblance to the four-note theme of the finale of the 'Jupiter' Symphony) which seem to go very well until they are chased away by those devilish ritornellos. The polyphonic writing is extremely complicated, but at the same time it is always light and natural. This extraordinary finale is brilliant proof of Mozart's complete success in accomplishing what he set out to do, to integrate the older style of music with that of the music of his day.

**Works written between December 31st, 1782 and June 17th, 1783**

*Scena and Rondo for soprano 'Mia speranza adorata',*
*K. 416*
*Arietta 'Männer suchen stets', K. 433*
*Aria for tenor 'Müsst ich auch', K. 435*
*Music to a pantomime, K. 446*
*Terzetto 'Das Bandel', K. 441*
*Piano Variations 'Salve tu, Domine', K. 398*
*Horn Concerto in E Flat Major, No. 2, K. 417*

# 8

# String Quartet in D Minor, K. 421 (Haydn No. 2)

1. **Allegro moderato**
2. **Andante in F Major**
3. **Minuet; trio in D Major**
4. **Allegro ma non troppo**

Constance became pregnant around the end of September 1782, which enabled Mozart to cite his wife's health as a reason for postponing his trip to Salzburg. While the first of the Haydn Quartets was being written, the Mozarts moved to another apartment on the Hohe Brücke. Their new apartment was roomier than their previous dwelling, but it proved to be beyond their means. In a letter to his father, Mozart described it as consisting of a main room '1000 feet long by 1 foot wide' (this was an old family joke), a bedroom, an antechamber and a large attractive kitchen, as well as two additional vacant rooms in which he gave a ball one evening in mid-January, 1783, which went on until seven o'clock the next morning.

January 27th, 1783, was Mozart's twenty-seventh birthday. Constanze was nineteen at the time. Both of them
were young and extravagant; they would never learn how
to live on a budget. Before long, they began to be harassed
by financial worries, from which they would never again
be free.

On February 4th, 'The Abduction from the Seraglio' was
performed for the seventeenth time, before a crowded audience.

Mozart had borrowed a large sum of money to pay for the
printing of some new concertos and his creditor began
demanding repayment. The young composer was panic-
stricken. He saw no way out other than to appeal to
Baroness Waldstädten, the lady who had given the dinner
in his honour on his wedding day. Naturally, Mozart
made no mention of this episode in his letters to Salzburg.
He did, however, urge his father to send him his Harlequin
costume as quickly as possible for a masked ball at the
Redoutensaal which he would attend together with his
sister-in-law Aloysia and her husband, Josef Lange. They
were to be dressed as Columbine and Pierrot.

On March 11th, Aloysia Lange gave a concert during which
Mozart was asked to play his first piano concerto, the Concerto in D Major, No. 5, K. 175, for which he had written
a new rondo, K. 382. A few days later, on the 23rd, Mozart
give a concert of his own with a very full programme.
Aloysia Lange and Valentin Adamberger (Belmonte in 'The
Abduction from the Seraglio') sang several arias. Mozart
conducted the 'Haffner' Symphony, and again played the

Concerto in D Major. He also played his new Piano Concerto in C. Major, No. 13, K. 415 a short fugue in honour of the Emperor, who was very fond of this form of composition (though hardly more so than Constanze); and, finally, two sets of Variations for piano, one of which delighted the audience so much that they insisted he play it again.

A letter received in Salzburg in May disclosed that Mozart and his wife had moved house twice since the beginning of the year. Baron Wetzlar, the owner of Herberstein House, at this time had taken a lady in to live with him. To oblige the Baron, the Mozarts left their apartment before their lease was up and moved into quite miserable lodgings on the Kohlmarkt. Baron Wetzlar refused to accept any rent for the three months the Mozarts spent in the apartment, and he even paid the cost of their move. Shortly afterward, they found suitable accommodation on the Judenplatz, on the second floor of the Burgischen House. It was here, on June 17th, during Constanze's confinement for the birth of their first son, Raimund Leopold, that Mozart wrote one of his most mournful compositions, the String Quartet in D Minor. This was the second in the series of six quartets dedicated to Haydn. As everyone busied themselves around the expectant mother, Mozart's nerves must have been strained, and understandably so. For all that, his new work betrayed a far deeper state of perturbation. In fact, long before Mozart penned the notes of the score, this quartet had been completed in his head. He was not 'composing' it he was 'writing' it. And for

Mozart there was all the difference in the world between the two.

Mozart never displayed any external signs of the deep psychological depression that held him in its grip during this period. He disciplined himself so as not to allow his private worries to interfere with his daily life or to become a source of embarrassment to those around him.

It would be interesting to know what his friends, his father and especially his dear friend Joseph Haydn thought of this piece of music, so utterly bereft of joy. The mood of sadness of the Quartet in D Minor is sustained from start to finish.

\* \* \*

**1. Allegro moderato** In this movement, everything seems to combine to create an impression of despair: the anguishing first subject, with its drop of one octave and its repeated trill; the feverishly insistent second subject; the tightly-knit counterpoint and incessant modulations; the complexity and length of the development section and, finally, the implacable brevity of the conclusion.

**2. Andante in F Major** This *andante* is not a true slow movement. (Nor, indeed, is there a true fast movement in this quartet: the first movement is marked *moderato;* the finale *ma non troppo.)* Here, the tone is one of sad, calm confidence. A central passage in A Major with a more urgent tempo allows the first violin to state an exquisite little phrase which is irresistibly graceful in its lightness. At bars 47 and 48 Mozart entrusts the first and second violins with three-note chords. As a general rule, he does this only to conclude a movement on a forceful note.)

**3. Minuet; trio in D Major**   In this movement the atmosphere of tension of the first movement is re-established. The minuet is an aggressive one, strangely wild and beautiful. The trio is highly original. Marked *sempre piano,* it unfolds in the style of a serenade against a background of pizzicatos (a technique which which was rarely used by Mozart).

**4. Allegro ma non troppo**   This movement consists of four variations and a coda on a theme which seems almost literally to gasp with anxiety. The rhythm is that of a *sicilienne.* Alhough the fourth variation is in D Major, the sense of sadness  remains unchanged. With the coda, the rhythm accelerates and the movement ends on a note of uncertainty in the anguished fluttering of repeated triplets.

# 1783 | 9 Mass in C Minor, K. 427

Mozart promised to go to Salzburg to have his thanksgiving mass sung. The occasion provided him with the opportunity to present Constanze to his father and sister.

On January 4th, 1783 he wrote to Leopold Mozart to explain:

"I made the promise in my heart of hearts and hope to be able to keep it. When I made it, my wife was not yet married; yet, as I was absolutely determined to marry her after her recovery, it was easy for me to make it — but as you yourself are aware, time and other circumstances made our journey impossible. The score of half of a mass, which is still lying here waiting to be finished, is the best proof that I really made the promise."

It was finally decided that they would leave for Salzburg at the end of July. Before departing, the Mozarts left their son, who was little more than a month old, not with his Grandmother Weber, but with a wet-nurse in the suburbs of Vienna.

Leopold Mozart and his daughter greeted the young couple cooly. Nannerl was then thirty-two years old and still unmarried. Perhaps she was a little jealous of her brother who had achieved success willy-nilly, while she (who could have become a great pianist) lived a boring life in Salzburg, giving piano lessons to preserve her independence.

As for Leopold, he felt no doubt bitter toward his ungrateful son whom he had nurtured so devotedly in his early years and who now rejected his father's sound advice and insisted on living his own life in his own way. Mozart was disappointed that his father made no move to give Constanze a family memento or one of the many presents which he himself had received as a child. Perhaps the only pleasure he derived from this visit to Salzburg (which was to be his last) was to see his old friends again. His friends, at least, thronged around, happy to reminisce with him about his days as an infant prodigy and to listen to him describing the success of 'The Abduction from the Seraglio' which they themselves had not yet heard. Mozart visited old Hagenauer, who still lived in the house in the Getreidegasse in which he had been born. He also visited Andreas Schachtner, Court trumpet-player and German translator of 'Idomeneo' and the Abbé Bullinger, to whom he had written immediately after his mother's death in Paris. And of course he visited Michael Haydn. Michael Haydn, Joseph's younger brother, had been Director of the Court orchestra and organist at the cathedral for nearly twenty years. Mozart respected him as a

# 1783

composer. Unfortunately, Haydn was unwell. Colloredo expected six duets for violin and viola from him but he had managed to finish only four. The Prince-Archbishop was becoming impatient and he threatened to cut off Haydn's salary to induce him to work. Mozart wrote the two remaining duets, partly to help his old friend and partly because the swindle was a way of getting even with his former master. Haydn submitted them to Colloredo with his own four as if nothing was amiss.

\*　\*　\*

In 1800, the publisher Johann Anton André (whom Mozart had met in Offenbach in 1790) paid Constanze 3150 florins (approximately $1,500) for 250 of her deceased husband's manuscripts. When he looked through the manuscript of the Mass in C Minor, he noticed that at least four sections of the 'Credo' were missing, as were the whole of the 'Agnus Dei' and the 'Dona nobis pacem'. He had only the 'Kyrie', the 'Gloria', two sections of the 'Credo' (and these not fully orchestrated), the 'Sanctus', and the 'Benedictus'. André asked Constanze why the work was incomplete. Mozart's widow advised him to seek the answer in Salzburg, where she recalled the mass has been "composed, or at any rate, performed".

We know now that this "score of half of a mass", mentioned earlier in Mozart's letter to his father, was written in Vienna in 1782. What we do not know is what Mozart intended when he left Vienna for Salzburg with his wife at the end of July 1783. Did he hope he could complete his work before it was to be sung? Perhaps he had long since decided to abandon it?

Since it is impossible to sing an unfinished mass, Mozart doubtless borrowed the missing parts from some of his earlier masses, for example, from his mass in C Minor, K. 138, a work of precocious maturity which he wrote in 1772. Perhaps for the 'Agnus Dei' he merely repeated, note for note, the music written for the 'Kyrie', as he was later to advise his pupil Süssmayr when he realized that his impending death would prevent him from finishing his 'Requiem'.

All that can be said with certainty is that the mass was rehearsed only once, an amazing feat for a work of this scope and complexity, on August 23rd. It was first performed, probably very poorly, two days later — not in the cathedral of his enemy Colloredo, but in the Church of St. Peter of Salzburg. The part of the first soprano was sung by Constanze Mozart.

\* \* \*

The Mass in C Minor is scored for two sopranos, tenor, bass, choir, organ and orchestra. The contrapuntal 'Kyrie' is a magnificent and solemn *andante moderato* in C Minor. The soprano's solo in the 'Christe eleison' is operatic in style. Mozart again uses the vocalizations he wrote for Constanze before their marriage, in which she was well practised.

The 'Gloria' is in seven sections. It begins with a grand chorus in C major, marked *allegro vivace*. It produces a

# 1783

brilliant effect, not unlike those of Handel's choruses which Mozart admired very much.

The double chorus for eight voices in G Minor, 'Qui tollis peccata mundi', is imposing in structure and entirely modern in its expression despite the use of the old-fashioned polyphonic style; it is the high point of the score. Indeed, some Mozartians firmly hold the opinion that this chorus should be classed as the equal of the best passages in Johann Sebastian Bach's Mass in B Minor.

The 'Jesu Christe' serves to introduce the beautiful, serene double fugue of the 'Cum spiritu'. The solo of the 'Laudeamus', the soprano duet of the 'Domine Deus' and the trio in the Italian style for two sopranos and tenor, the 'Quoniam tu solus', all seem somewhat shallow by comparison.

As can be seen, the Mass in C Minor is made up of many different elements. The second section of the 'Credo', the 'Et incarnatus est', is a piece of bravura for soprano heavy with rich Italianate ornamentation. To the pious citizens of Salzburg, it may well have seemed scandalously frivolous. Be that as it may, there is no denying that this worldly, graceful Christmas carol, so exquisitely Mozartian in character, so delicately written and with such limpid resonance in the obbligato from the wind instruments, is endowed with an irresistible charm.

In the 'Sanctus', a chorus in C Major introduces the double fugue for eight voices, 'Hosanna in excelsis'; it is a grandiose and complex piece of music.

The 'Benedictus' is a quartet for two sopranos, tenor and bass.

Mozart's manuscript ends with the double fugue 'Hosanna in excelsis', another excellent example of counterpoint stripped of all possible opacity.

**Works written between August 25th, 1783 and January, 1784**

*Duets for violin and viola:*
— *in G Major, K. 423*
— *in B Flat Major, K. 424*
*Symphony in C Major, No. 36, K. 425 ('Linz')*
*Introduction to a symphony in G Major by Michael Haydn, K. 444*
*'L'Oca del Cairo', K. 422*
*Aria for tenor 'Misero, o sogno!', K. 431*
*Aria for bass 'Cosi dunque tradisci', K. 432*
*Fugue for two pianos in C Minor, K. 426*
*Horn Concerto in E Flat Major, No. 3, K. 447*

# 10

# String Quartet in E Flat Major, (Haydn No. 3)

1. **Allegro non troppo**
2. **Andante con moto in A Flat Major**
3. **Minuet; trio in B Flat Major**
4. **Allegro vivace**

While Mozart was in Salzburg rehearsing and directing his Mass in C Minor, his son, Raimund Leopold died of dysentery in Vienna. By the time he and Constanze received the news, the child had already been buried. Perhaps because there was hardly any incentive for either of them to return to their apartment, now that their son was no longer there, they stayed in Salzburg for three months.

At the end of October, Mozart left the city where he had been born. He was never to return.

On the way back to Vienna, the Mozarts stopped at Linz, where Count Thun welcomed them warmly. To please the Count, Mozart wrote a symphony in four days and dedicated it to him; the Symphony in C Major, No. 36, K. 425.

Mozart and his wife returned to Vienna at the end of November. They were anxious to leave the apartment where they were haunted by the memory of their dead son. Before very long they moved to an apartment in the Graben, on the fourth floor of a house owned by the publisher Johann Thomas von Trattner, whose wife Therese was a pupil of Mozart's.

In January 1784, Mozart completed the third of the Haydn Quartets, the Quartet in E Flat Major, K. 428. That year, and the one following were to prove splendidly successful for him.

On January 27th he celebrated his twenty-eighth birthday. Constanze was again pregnant; the baby was expected at the end of September.

*     *     *

1. **Allegro non troppo** The opening theme, questioning and mysterious, is stated in unison by the quartet. The question is posed for a second time by the four instruments, but this time amid the confusion of a surprising outburst of discords. There is no true sadness in this movement and no true joy. There is rather a note of solemnity and a deep warmth of expression. A very short development

is carried over into the recapitulation, one of Mozart's favourite practices.

**2. Andante con moto in A Flat Major**   This is a meditation, 96 bars in length, which exhibits great harmonic richness. Rather than an actual theme, Mozart propounds a series of syncopations with an accompaniment in 6/8 time from the violoncello, thus creating a dark and heavy mood. The development section of this sonata-form movement is also very short, but it has a gripping effect. Mozart makes use of little impressionistic touches including dissonances and chromatic effects. After a series of poignant chords, the movement brightens up, ending in a most wonderfully satisfying fashion.

**3. Minuet; trio in B Flat Major**   A forceful, heavily accented minuet. Mozart makes use of hurdy-gurdy and canonic effects. The sad, tender theme of the trio, which is introduced in C Minor, is written in the key of B Flat Major. In the end, it flows back to its true tonality with remarkable ease.

**4. Allegro vivace**   The first subject of this rondo is a dry, insistent motif which ends in a mad rush. The second subject serves to introduce a magnificent theme (bar 60) which is, at one and the same time, lyrical and vivacious, light and full of power. It is repeated by Mozart in the recapitulation, but this time it is distinctively more sombre in character, having modulated to a lower register. This is a typical Mozartian change of mood. The entire movement is full of activity. The coda is delightful in its simplicity, although Mozart seems a little in a rush to get it over with.

## Works written in January 1784

*5 Minuets for orchestra, K. 461*
*6 Contredanses for orchestra, K. 462*
*2 Minuets with contredanses for orchestra, K. 463*

# 11

## 1784

# Concerto for piano and orchestra in E Flat Major, No. 14 K. 449

1. **Allegro vivace**
2. **Andantino in B Flat Major**
3. **Allegro ma non troppo**

On his return to Vienna, Mozart resumed his teaching and the instruction of pupils who represented his bread and butter. He also threw himself into the preparations for his new concert season.

He adopted the excellent practice of describing each of his compositions in an unpretentions exercise-book, which had a blue cover decorated with little flowers. In the left-hand page he wrote the composition's date of completion, its instrumentation, the names of the performers and the person to whom the work was dedicated as applicable. On the right-hand page he carefully reproduced the opening bars.

The first work which appears in this book is dated February 4th, 1784. It is the Concerto for piano and orchestra in E Flat Major, K. 449, and is dedicated to Barbara Ployer, a new pupil who came from Salzburg. The last work noted by Mozart in this catalogue is his Masonic cantata 'Das Lob der Freundschaft', K. 623 (In Praise of Friendship), which was completed on November 15th, 1791, twenty-three days before his death.

In a letter to his father, written a few days after he completed the Concerto in E Flat Major, Mozart came out with this cry from the heart:

"If you could only hear what I've composed! I spend the whole morning giving lessons so I have only the evening for my beloved task — composition."

Between February 26th and April 3rd, Mozart participated in no fewer than twenty-one concerts which he called 'academien'. He had every right to complain.

"Well, haven't I enough to do? I don't think in this way I can possibly get out of practice."

A Dutch pianist named Richter invited him to take part in three of his own 'academien'. Mozart reported how much the virtuoso admired his facility at the piano and how, when he heard him play, he would keep repeating: " 'Good God! How hard I work and sweat — and yet win no applause — and to you, my friend, it is all child's play.' 'Yes' I replied, 'I too had to work hard, so as not to have to work hard any longer'."

"If you could only hear what I've composed — ! " Mozart had the right to be proud of his Concerto in E Flat Major. Conceived in a new style, it inaugurated the grandiose cycle of his Viennese concertos, fourteen compositions, some ten of which are perhaps the most beautiful examples of his instrumental work.

Mozart's next three concertos, sometimes described as 'grand concertos' in recognition of the fact that the Concerto in E Flat Major belongs (as Mozart himself expressly stated) " . . . not . . . at all to the same category. It is one of a quite peculiar kind, composed rather for a small orchestra than for a large one." The accompaniment is, as a matter of fact, for strings with two oboes and two horns ad libitum. It goes without saying that the presence of these optional oboes and horns enriches the orchestral texture of the concerto.

During this one year, 1784, Mozart composed six piano concertos. The following year he wrote another three; and three more in 1786. These three years are the ones of his great Viennese successes as a pianist and as a composer of piano concertos.

After 1786, the Viennese seemed to tire somewhat of the virtuoso and his concertos, and Mozart stopped writing them. Subsequently, he composed only two more, the Concerto in D Major, No. 26, K. 537, known as the 'Coronation' Concerto, written in 1788, and the last of the series, the Concerto in B Flat Major, No. 27, K. 595, in January 1791,

In Mozartian terms, a piano concerto can be described more or less as follows: a first movement, symphonic in nature, intended to evoke surprise and interest; a slow movement, more intimate, aimed at charming the listener and arousing his emotions; and an animated finale, the objective of which is to amuse the listener — and which may go as far as buffoonery to achieve that objective.

The fourteen great concertos written in Vienna each have these three characteristics in common, in one way or another. There are, however, marked differences between them with regard to colour, expression and character.

\*   \*   \*

**1. Allegro vivace**   As the orchestra propounds, in unison, the wonderful winding first theme of this movement, one's first impression is that it is written in a minor key. An impressive symphonic prelude establishes a melancholy mood which the piano seeks in vain to dispel by dint of sheer optimistic energy. The rhythmic evolution of the movement is somewhat whimsical, and gives rise to a feeling of instability. Despite the marking *vivace,* the pace of this *allegro* is singularly devoid of lightness.

**2. Andantino in B Flat Major**   This is a magnificent song of great expressiveness. The delivery, which approaches that of human speech, reminds one of the recitative episodes in the *andantino* of the 'Jeunehomme' Concerto.

**3. Allegro ma non troppo**   This elegant final rondo, interwoven with contrapuntal elements, is a constant source of joy for the soloist. From the moment the piano comes in, it is kept in a perpetual motion. The single theme is repeated constantly, with variations of never-failing imagination. Near the end, the theme changes from its previous march time to a 6/8 rhythm and becomes a dance.

Concerto for piano and orchestra in
E Flat Major, No. 14, K. 449

**Works written between February 9th
and March 30th, 1784**

*Concertos for piano and orchestra:*
    *— in B Flat Major, No. 15, K. 450*
    *— in D Major, No. 16, K. 451*

# 12
# Quintet for wind instruments and piano in E Flat Major, K. 452

## 1784

1. Largo; allegro moderato
2. Larghetto in B Flat Major
3. Allegretto

At this time, Mozart scarcely had a moment's peace. His pupils took up his every morning, his concerts every evening. How did he find time to write his new works? Undoubtedly at night, which he preferred to the daytime for composition in any case.

On April 10th, he told his father he had written two grand piano concertos (one in B Flat Major, K. 450 and one in D Major, K. 451), which he described as being absolutely guaranteed to "make the performer perspire". Then he added:

"... and then a quintet, which called forth the very greatest applause: I myself consider it to be the best work

*Mozart at the piano, about 1783.*
*Unfinished painting by Josef Lange,*
*Mozart's brother-in-law.*

I have ever composed. It is written for one oboe, one clarinet, one horn, one bassoon and the pianoforte. How I wish you could have heard it! And how beautifully it was performed! Well, to tell the truth I was really worn out in the end after playing so much — and it is greatly to my credit that my listeners never got tired."

The portrait of Mozart, begun by his brother-in-law Josef Lange in the winter of 1782, was never finished. It shows the composer seated at the piano without his wig. There is a look of concentration on his face and his mouth has a serious set to it. It shows his prominent nose and his head which, in terms of proportion, appears to have been too big for his body. This is the most famous of the many portraits of Mozart, all of which are strangely contradictory.

\* \* \*

Mozart had not previously composed a quintet especially for wind instruments and piano. This, his first attempt, is a masterpiece and is unforgettable for the sound it produces. Mozart, however, does not involve his inner self in this work as intimately as he does in his string quartets. The Quintet for wind instruments and piano in E Flat Major is a sort of chamber sinfonia concertante — young, fresh, vigorous and obviously intended to create a stir.

**1. Largo; allegro moderato** A slow, short and solemn introduction, which is splendidly resonant, leads into a good-natured *allegro moderato* which makes use of all sorts of instrumental combinations. Each instrumentalist takes the lead in turn, although none of them is permitted to outshine the others. Mozart writes beautifully for wind instruments. He knows how to make them sing (and also catch their breath) with consummate artisty.

**2. Larghetto in B Flat Major**   The movement begins in a calm and dignified manner. The action slowly builds to a climax, during which Mozart ventures an astonishing series of modulations: arpeggios on the piano against a background of sustained chords from the winds. These daring harmonies must have amazed all those who heard them for the first time, their effect is truly electrifying. In the coda, there are fresh shocks from a series of equally unusual dissonant chords. The movement ends as it began, in peace and calm.

**3. Allegretto**   A rondo bubbling over with gaiety brings one of Mozart's happiest compositions to an end. The high point of the movement is the marvellous cadenza during which the five instrumentalists indulge themselves to their heart's content, each trying to outdo the others' virtuosity.

# 13

# 1784 | Concerto for piano and orchestra in G Major, No. 17, K. 453

1. **Allegro**
2. **Andante in C Major**
3. **Allegretto; presto**

The Viennese concert season was in full swing, and Mozart could no longer find even a minute to write to his father. After three weeks of silence, he was finally able to pen a note on April 10th.

"Please don't be vexed that I haven't written to you for so long. Surely you realise how much I have to do in the meantime!"

He did, however, find time to help a young violinist, Franz Menzel, obtain a position with the Salzburg orchestra. He recommended Menzel very highly to his father, pointing out that he had managed to play Mozart's three recent string quartets at sight, a remarkable feat! He added, not without humour, that he had begged the young man never to mention the name 'Wolfgang Mozart' in Salzburg. To do so might well prove fatal to him!

It was not within Mozart to withhold recognition of a genuine talent, and in another letter to his father he also praised several quartets which had recently been circulated over the signature of Ignaz Joseph Pleyel, one of Haydn's pupils.

"They are very well written and most pleasing to listen to. You will also see at once who was his master. Well, it will be a lucky day for music if later on Pleyel should be able to replace Haydn."

On April 12th, Mozart finished a second piano concerto written for his pupil Barbara ('Babette') Ployer — the dazzling Concerto in G Major, No. 17, K. 453, which is certainly the most uninterruptedly happy of all his piano concertos.

When Mozart died in 1791 at the age of thirty-five, he had completed more than six hundred compositions. Although Mozart experienced periods of crisis, during which he wrote relatively little, these were comparatively rare. In fact, through the whole of his life, he never stopped writing music.

On top of his immense creative effort must be added the fatigue of the lessons he gave, his concerts, the many moves of dwelling, his tours, his heavy correspondence (more than four hundred letters) and a thousand and one domestic chores. One can only arrive at the inevitable conclusion that Mozart simply never took any time to rest.

To illustrate his unceasing activity, the following is a list of the works produced by Mozart during the year 1784.

| | |
|---|---|
| In January : | 5 Minuets for orchestra, K. 461; 6 Contre-danses for orchestra, K. 462; 2 Minuets with Contredanses for orchestra, K. 463. |
| February 9th: | Piano Concerto in E Flat Major, No. 14, K. 449 |
| March 15th: | Piano Concerto in B Flat Major, No. 15, K. 450 |
| March 22nd: | Piano Concerto in D Major, No. 16, K. 451 |
| March 30th: | Quintet for wind instruments and piano in E Flat Major, K. 452 |
| April 12th: | Piano Concerto in G Major, No. 17, K. 453 |
| April 29th: | Sonata for violin and piano in B Flat Major, K. 454 |
| In June: | Piano Variations in A Major, K. 460 |
| August 25th: | Piano Variations in G Major, K. 455 |
| September 30th: | Piano Concerto in B Flat Major, No. 18, K. 456 |
| October 14th: | Piano Sonata in C Minor, K. 457 |
| November 9th: | String Quartet in B Flat Major, K. 458 |
| December 11th: | Piano Concerto in F Major, No. 19, K. 459 |

After having completed two major piano concertos and a quintet for piano and winds, all within the space of two weeks, Mozart had every reason for his outburst in his letter to his father of April 10th — "Surely you realize how much I have to do in the meantime!"

\* \* \*

**1. Allegro**  Gaiety sparkles from the very beginning of the exposition. The thematic material is rich and varied and the dialogue between the soloist and the orchestra is particularly warm. The writing is delicate clear and very elegant. Mozart wrote two cadenzas for this movement. (It is interesting to note that the first subject of the movement is rhythmically identical wih those of three other concertos written in 1784: K. 451, K. 456 and K. 459.)

**2. Andante in C Major**  This *andante* devotes itself to a pleasing task, that of supplying answers to a question posed by the orchestra at the beginning of the movement. Each answer seems even more enchanting than the last. The conversation between the piano and the orchestra is incomparably shy and tender.

**3. Allegretto; presto**  On January 1st, 1784, Mozart started recording his expenses in a notebook which also contained some English exercises, but which he stopped using after only a few months. On May 27th he noted: "One singing starling — 34 kreutzers". Beside this entry he wrote down the bird's song, in G Major, with the words "How beautiful it was!" The initial theme of the finale derives from that starling's song. Mozart turns it into a little tune, in the spirit of a German folk-song, followed by five variations. He then speeds up the tempo and launches into a stirring coda filled with clownery. At certain moments the woodwinds seem literally to guffaw with laughter, like a band of urchins. In the end, their mirth infects the entire orchestra.

The singing starling died in June, 1787. Mozart buried it in his garden, with a short epitaph in verse.

**Works written between April 12th and October 14th, 1784**

*Sonata for violin and piano in B Flat Major, K. 454*
*Piano Variations:*
  *— in A Major, K. 460*
  *— in G Major, K. 455*
*Piano Concerto in B Flat Major, No. 18, K. 456*

# 14

## 1784 | Piano Sonata in C Minor, K. 457

1. Allegro molto
2. Adagio in E Flat Major
3. Allegro assai

Mozart's lovely Sonata in B Flat Major, K. 454, was written for Regina Strinasacchi, the celebrated violinist from Mantua. By the evening of the concert, on April 29th, 1784, Mozart had not found time to write any of the score except the part of the violin itself. He played the piano part entirely from memory, much to the astonishment of the Emperor, whose opera-glasses revealed that Mozart had placed a blank sheet of paper on the piano in front of him. It was not until after the concert that Mozart managed to complete the score.

This incident illustrates very clearly what Mozart meant when he said that he had 'composed' a work, but had not yet 'written' it.

Relaxing after his prodigious efforts of the spring season,

he stopped working on his compositions during the earlier part of the summer. His students were away for their holidays and he had a little spare time at last. In the mornings, he went riding in the Augarten between 6 and 8 a.m. In the afternoons he went for walks with Constanze or played billiards with his friends in the apartment on the Graben.

At this time, Mozart renewed his acquaintance with Giovanni Paisiello, whom he had met in Italy in 1770: Paisiello had recently returned from an eight-year stay in St. Petersburg where his 'Barber of Seville' had been performed at the court of Catherine II of Russia. Paisiello was then completing a new opera for Vienna — 'Il Re Teodoro in Venezia'. The two men thought a good deal of each other and they never tired of discussing opera in all its aspects.

Mozart's love of the theatre is well known. All through his life he constantly sought opportunities to write for this medium. "He always has an opera in his head", Leopold wrote of him in May, 1769, when his son was only thirteen years old.

Mozart had considered three operas since 1783: 'L'Oca del Cairo', 'Lo Sposo deluso' and 'Il Regno delle Amazone'. After several rough drafts, however, he rejected all three of them because of their poor librettos.

In August, it was suddenly announced that Nannerl was to marry Johann Baptist von Berchthold zu Sonnenburg, a widower of 48 with five children. The newly-weds were to live at St. Gilgen, near Salzburg, in the very same house

*Maria Anna (Nannerl)*
*von Berchthold.  About 1785.*

where Anna Maria Mozart had been born.

Mozart did not attend his sister's wedding. He contented himself with writing her a letter of good wishes in which he included the usual comic 'advice to the bride' and promised to send her a handsome apron from Constanze by the following post.

No trace has been found of any of Mozart's letters to his family from the time of this letter to Nannerl dated August 18th, 1784, and his letter to his father dated April 4th, 1787 (written in response to the news he had just received of his father's serious illness which was to carry him off less than two months later). There is reason to believe that some of these letters were deliberately destroyed because they dealt with Mozart's initiation into Freemasonry in December 1784.

Some of them, but what of the others? Nannerl perhaps gave Mozart back several bundles of his letters after their father's death in May 1787, only to have him lose them later on during one of his many changes of address, but this is speculation.

On the other hand, we do have a letter written by Leopold to his daughter on September 14th, 1784, telling her that Wolfgang had been taken seciously ill in Vienna. He suddenly begun perspiring so profusely during a performance of Paisiello's opera that before long he had to leave the theatre with his clothing soaked completely through. For four days he suffered violent attacks of colic and vomiting. Had it not been for his friend Dr. Sigmund Barisani, it is doubtful that he would be alive today, said Leopold.

# 1784

It is likely that Mozart was not recovered by September 21st, the day of the birth of his second child, Karl Thomas. The child's godfather was Johann von Trattner, the publisher and bookseller, whose wife Therese had been a pupil of Mozart for the previous three years.

The remaining months of 1784 are clouded in mystery as far as Mozart and his family are concerned.
Suddenly, around the end of September, the Mozarts moved house again, this time to Schulerstrasse. What happened? Did Constanze suddenly become jealous of the relationship between the master and his pupil? Did von Trattner make a scene about it? We do not know.

On October 14th, however, we do know that Mozart finished the Sonata in C Minor which he dedicated to Therese von Tratter. This mournful piece of music shows how distressed and out of sorts Mozart must have been when he wrote it. Again, for reasons we do not know, when Mozart published this sonata in May, 1785, he preceded it by a Fantasia in C Minor which he also dedicated to Frau von Trattner.

After Mozart's death, Constanze asked Therese to return some letters Mozart had written her which contained invaluable instructions as to how the sonata should be played. Therese von Trattner maintained she had lost the letters, and to this day they have never been seen.

\* \* \*

**1. Allegro molto**  It has often been said that this movement anticipates Beethoven's sonatas by its sheer breadth
of range. It is, however, typically Mozartian nervous
energy that makes it so dramatic rather than the passion
associated with Beethoven. Indeed, its whole content
seems to consist entirely of fever, sadness, bitterness and
anguished cries from the heart. The monumental coda
ends with ten enigmatic bars of astounding brevity.

**2. Adagio in E Flat Major**  The melodies which unfold
during the course of this great lyrical movement are repeated several times, each time with a different décor. In the
last three bars, pulsing demi-semiquavers provide a fore-
warning of the disturbing breathless gasps of the final
rondo.

**3. Allegro assai**  The finale is punctuated by violent
outburst and the fabric is slashed with brutal interruptions
and fermatas. As with the first movement, the ending is
so unexpected that the listener finds himself left with a
vague feeling of emotional distress.

# 15

## 1784 | String Quartet in B Flat Major, K. 458 (Haydn No. 4)

1. Allegro vivace assai
2. Minuet and trio: moderato
3. Adagio in E Flat Major
4. Allegro assai

In the early autumn of 1784, Mozart prepared for his second Viennese season. As with the previous season, he organized subscription concerts, but this time he planned to give them not in the large hall of the von Trattner house where he lived, but in an even larger room in the Mehlgrube.

On Sunday mornings, Mozart often attended concerts of polyphonic music given at the house of Baron van Swieten. On Sunday afternoons, he played music at home. On these occasions, the publisher, Hoffmeister, was often in attendance, as was a young English singer of nineteen, Anna Selina Storace (who was always called Nancy), and her brother, Stephen Storace, the composer who was one of Mozart's pupils.

Beside the Storaces, Mozart made two more new friends in Vienna, Thomas Attwood, who became one of his favourite pupils, and the Irish tenor, Michael Kelly, with whom he liked to play billiards and who had just come from Italy where he had been pursuing his career under the name of Ocheli.

Before long, Nancy Storace would play the role of Susanna in 'The Marriage of Figaro', with Kelly as Basilio and Don Curzio.

Kelly has left us some invaluable memoirs which are full of references to Mozart.

To these young musicians, Mozart was not only a master who had already had a career spanning twenty-three years, despite the fact that he was not much older than they themselves. He was something more; an artist who outstripped them all with his genius and his experience of life and people. And to top it all off, Mozart loved to have a good time so, naturally, the bonds between them were extremely friendly.

For his Sunday chamber music sessions, Mozart finished the fourth of the Haydn Quartets on November 9th, 1784. Known as 'The Hunt' Quartet, it was the Quartet in B Flat Major, K. 458.

**1. Allegro vivace assai** This quartet is known as 'The Hunt' Quartet because of the gay fanfare introduced in the first frisky subject. It is one of the most joyous themes that Mozart ever wrote. The second subject is a group of five quick notes, interrupted by pauses. After the double bar there is an exquisite melody, derived from the first

*Nancy Storace. After an
engraving by Betttelini.*

subject, but Mozart abandons it after sixteen bars in favour of the five-note *gruppetto* which forms most of the brief development. During the recapitulation, and especially during the lenthy coda, Mozart again presents his thematic material in a different guise.

**2. Minuet and trio: moderato**   The offbeat accentuation of this solemn minuet endows it with a limping gait. The trio, which makes a graceful counterpart, dances along a little more freely, although it never completely sheds its somewhat formal nature.

**3. Adagio in E Flat Major**   This is a moving song, punctuated with rests and calls. Mozart whispers sad secrets in our ear during this movement, offering a striking contrast to the two that precede it. There is seemingly a kind of private understanding between the first violin and the violoncello. This is the only *adagio* in any of the Haydn Quartets.

**4. Allegro assai**   This is a movement in sonata-form comprising three well-defined subjects and punctuated by imperious utterances. The mood is feverish rather than truly lively.

**Sole work written between November 9th, 1784 and January 10th, 1785**

*Piano Concerto in F Major, No. 19, K. 459*

# 16

## 1785 | String Quartet in A Major, K. 464 (Haydn No. 5)

1. Allegro
2. Minuet; trio in E Major
3. Andante in D Major
4. Allegro

'The Abduction from the Seraglio' continued its brilliant course. It was sung in Mannheim, Mainz and Berlin. Finally, on November 17th, 1784, it was enthusiastically received in Salzburg.

The entire city seemed enchanted with it. Even Colloredo himself condescended to admit that the opera was "not bad". Mozart's father and Michael Haydn were delighted.

In Vienna that December, Mozart wrote only one work, the Piano Concerto in F Major, No. 19, K. 459, which he finished on the 11th.

On the 14th, Wolfgang Amadeus Mozart, whose fondest dreams never ceased to include friendship and love of mankind, was initiated into Freemasonry as an apprentice in the lodge of 'The New-Crowned Hope'.

Mozart was doubtless not a devout Catholic, although he never lost his faith. On the other hand, he was a zealous Freemason. There was nothing incongruous in his opinion in believing in Holy Church and being a Masonic brother at the same time. It has often been pointed out that this same sincere religious sentiment is found both in the motet 'Ave verum corpus' and in the masonic hymn 'O, Isis und Osiris' from 'The Magic Flute'.

Mozart must have found it difficult to understand the Church's hostility toward a society which preached the happiness of mankind, brotherhood, wisdom and serenity in the face of death. He numbered friends and acquaintances among his fellow Masons, drawn from every class of society. Inside the lodge, this man who had to suffer the contempt of the likes of Colloredo and Arco must have felt himself revenged when he found himself on an equal footing with the great ones of the earth.

At the outset of the French Revolution, Freemasons were accused of having plotted the downfall of monarchy. Like all the other Masons in Vienna, Mozart became a suspect in the eyes of the nobility and the clergy. This added to making the last years of his life even more miserable.

In January, 1785, Mozart completed the Haydn Quartets at four day intervals. The fifth in the series, the Quartet in A Major, K. 464, was dated January 10th; the sixth was completed on January 14th.

When Leopold Mozart heard these two quartets in his son's lodgings in Vienna a month later, he described them to his daughter as being "somewhat easier, but at the same time excellent compositions" — by which he meant their

118

conception was clearer, their style less ornate their understanding less arduous than the first of the series.

The fifth Haydn Quartet was Mozart's first composition
after his initiation into Freemasony. This is perhaps why
Mozart wrote it in A Major, a key having three sharps —
three being the cipher-figure of Masonic symbolism.

\* \* \*

**1. Allegro**   This is the most peaceful *allegro* in all the
six quartets of the series, expressing as it does a happiness
entirely devoid of passion. Except for one or two moments
of agitation during the development, the tone remains
noble and detached throughout the entire movement.
The gracefulness with which the contrapuntal elements
are treated here is quite refreshing.

**2. Minuet; trio in E Major**   The minuet, which uses
polyphonic elements, is sombre and severe and creates a
curious impression of immobility. In contrast, the trio
(written in the rare key of E Major) is airy and light and
completely charming.

**3. Andante in D Major**   Here Mozart uses a march theme
as the source for six of his best varitions. The astonishing
flexibility of the first of these reminds one of the opening
theme of the first of the Haydn Quartets, K. 387. The
second variation is lyrical; the third is rhythmic. The fourth
variation takes the form of a moving song in D Minor. We
return to the lighter mood of D Major for the fifth variation,
which is contrapuntal. At the outset of the fifth, the cello
begins to hammer out an *ostinato* rhythm which soon
pervades the other instruments. A startling effect.

119

**4. Allegro** After stating a short, abrupt and resolute first subject, this movement in sonata-form leads to a central episode during which the whole quartet launches into a magnificent and unsuspected hymn in D Major. Beethoven thought so highly of this piece that he made a copy of it in his own hand.

# 17

## 1785 | String Quartet in C Major, K. 465 (Haydn No. 6)

1. **Adagio; allegro**
2. **Andante cantabile in F Major**
3. **Minuet; trio in C Minor**
4. **Allegro**

On January 14th, 1785, Mozart wrote the last of the six Haydn Quartets: the Quartet in C Major K. 465.

The series had begun in the joy and enthusiasm of the discovery of a new style. It ended in a supreme display of sensitivity and intelligence. The quartets were published by Artaria in September 1785, with the following dedication to Joseph Haydn written in Italian by Mozart:

"To my dear friend Haydn.

"A father who had decided to send out his sons into the great world, thought it his duty to entrust them to the protection and guidance of a man who was very celebrated at the time and who, moreover, happened to be his best friend.

SEI
QUARTETTI
PER DUE VIOLINI, VIOLA, E VIOLONCELLO.

Composti e Dedicati
al Signor

GIUSEPPE HAYDN

Maestro di Cappella di S.A.
il Principe d'Esterhazy &c &c

Dal Suo Amico

W.A.MOZART
Opera X.

In Vienna presso Artaria Comp.
Mercanti d'Editori di Stampe Musica,
e Carte Geografiche

*Title-page of the first*
*edition of Mozart's*
*six string quartets*
*dedicated to Joseph Haydn.*

"In like manner I send my six sons to you, most celebrated and very dear friend. They are, indeed, the fruit of a long and laborious study; but the hope which many friends have given me that this toil will be in some degree rewarded, encourages me and flatters me with the thought that these children may one day prove a source of consolation to me.

"During your last stay in this capital, you yourself, my very dear friend, expressed to me your approval of these compositions. Your good opinion encourages me to offer them to you and leads me to hope that you will not consider them wholly unworthy of your favour. Please then receive them kindly and be to them a father, guide and friend! From this moment I surrender to you all my rights over them. I entreat you, however, to be indulgent to those faults which may have escaped a father's partial eye, and, in spite of them, to continue your generous friendship towards one who so highly appreciates it. Meanwhile, I remain with all my heart, dearest friend, your most sincere friend.

W. A. MOZART"

Mozart always said that Joseph Haydn was the only musician he knew to whom he could have dedicated his new quartets for the simple reason that it was from Haydn that he had learned how to write them. "Nobody," he would say, "knows as well as Haydn how to move a man or how to make him laugh."

When Artaria sent the Haydn Quartets to Italy, they were returned on the grounds that they were full of printing

*Joseph Haydn.*

errors. For some time to come the discords, which are scattered abundantly throughout these works, would be mistaken for errors. It was to be a long time, indeed, before their boldness and novelty would succeed in arousing anything but difference and incomprehension from the public.

\*    \*    \*

The Quartet in C Major is referred to as the "Dissonant Quartet". The clashes of harmony which occur at the beginning of the *adagio* do indeed produce a disturbing impression of atonality. False relations were used in music well before Mozart's time. However, those in this quartet were initially considered to be errors. Indeed, the 19th-Century Belgian musicologist, François-Joseph Fétis, even affirmed one day that he felt it his duty to "correct" them.

**1. Adagio; allegro**   The twenty-two bars of this meditative *adagio* create such an atmosphere of anticipation that at first the listener is deceived by the apparently casual mood of the *allegro*. After the double bar, however, Mozart offers us one of the most astonishing passages of thematic development in the whole series of the Haydn Quartets: fifty bars of modulations and marvellous imitation drawn from the first subject. The movement ends simply and *pianissimo*.

**2. Andante cantabile in F Major**   A cantilena of exquisite design leads to a little rhythmic figure which the first violin and the violoncello bandy back and forth in melancholy fashion throughout the movement. This *andante* exudes a spell-binding and ecstatic charm.

**3. Minuet; trio in C Minor**   This is a robust and insistant minuet with a distinctively chromatic flavour. The trio is excitable, animated by an earnest, almost emphatic passion. There is nothing restful in this movement.

**4. Allegro**   The finale is marked by great activity. The first two subjects, although lively and decisive, are not particularly remarkable. The third, in E Flat Major (Bars 89 to 104) is sung by the two violins, playing octaves, against a bouncing accompaniment provided by the viola and the cello. This is the crowning jewel of the whole movement. It offers a moment of infinite tenderness and pure emotion. The development is tense, strengthened by counterpoint and slashed with bars of rest. During the recapitulation, Mozart repeats the third subject for us, this time in A Flat Major, and gives it a brief canonic ending.   This dazzlingly imaginative movement brings the Haydn Quartet series to an end.

# 18
## 1785 | Concerto for piano and orchestra in D Minor, No. 20, K. 466

1. **Allegro**
2. **Romanza in B Flat Major**
3. **Allegro assai**

On Friday, February 11th, 1785, Leopold Mozart arrived in Vienna accompanied by his brilliant violinist-pupil, Heinrich Marchand. Leopold was to remain until April 25th.

Mozart's father entered the house at 1 p.m., just as Mozart was handing over the last pages of his Concerto in D Minor to the copyist. He had only just finished the work which he was scheduled to play that very evening in the Mehlgrube Theatre. He had been in such a hurry to finish it that he did not even take time to run over the final rondo on the piano. That same day, father and son attended the ceremony at which Joseph Haydn was initiated into Freemasonry.

That evening, Leopold Mozart attended the first of the subscription concerts which his son had arranged to give during the 1785 Carnival. He found the orchestra excellent and the new concerto magnificent.

The next day, which was a Saturday, there was a musical evening at Mozart's house. In his first letter to Nannerl from Vienna, written on February 16th, Leopold wrote: ". . . Herr Joseph Haydn and the two Barons Tinti came to see us and the new quartets were performed, or rather, the three new ones which Wolfgang has added to the other three which we have already. The new ones are somewhat easier, but at the same time excellent compositions. Haydn said to me: 'Before God and as an honest man I tell you that your son is the greatest composer known to me either in person or by name. He has taste and, what is more, the most profound knowledge of composition'."

It seems clear that Haydn must have been moved to say this by the very strong emotions he had felt the evening before when he first heard the Concerto in D Minor. He alone had understood its grandeur and its originality.

As for Leopold Mozart, in his letter of February 16th to his daughter telling her about the concerto, he shows no surprise at the pathos of the first movement, although this is very evident. Nor does he mention the key, which is one rarely used for a concerto.

On February 13th, Mozart took part in the 'academie' of the Italian singer Luisa Laschi (who was later to become the Countess in 'The Marriage of Figaro'). He played his Piano Concerto in B Flat Major, No. 18, K. 456, which was composed for the blind virtuoso, Maria Theresia Paradis. Up in his box, the Emperor waved his hat and shouted: "Bravo, Mozart!"

\*    \*    \*

The Concerto in D Minor was the first of two piano concertos which Mozart wrote in a minor key; the second was the Concerto in C Minor, No. 24, K. 491, which is finished on March 24th, 1786.

The fiery excitement of these concertos stemmed from a transitory mood. Once Mozart had rid himself of it, he reverted to his true self — a temperate, disciplined, 18th Century artist, incapable of excess — the "composer who has taste" Haydn had spoken of to Leopold.

It is interesting, nevertheless, to note that for a fleeting moment Mozart experienced the fever that would soon sweep over Europe, and that some of his works would blaze the trail for German romantic music.

In the 19th Century, the Concerto in D Minor was the most popular of Mozart's piano concertos. This is still the case today. Beethoven thought very highly of this concerto and wrote a beautiful cadenza for it in a style that is a blend of Mozart's and his own.

\*    \*    \*

**1. Allegro** The powerful orchestral introduction to this concerto unfolds in uncertainty and gloom. It charges the atmosphere with apprehension. Several themes are announced before the piano makes its entry with a new theme that is never taken up by the orchestra. The solo and the *tutti* confront each other with tireless energy. *Sturm und Drang.* Storm and stress. *Tourmente et poussée de passion.*

**2. Romanza in B Flat Major**   This slow movement is, strictly speaking, a rondo. At the outset the piano starts off alone, singing a song of divine beauty which is then taken up by the orchestra. Piano and orchestra converse together. The impression is one of a blue sky, soothing and fragrant air, and a countryside at rest. Suddenly, a storm appears, (episode in G Minor) swirling in a veritable paroxysm of despair. The storm passes and we return to serenity with a coda of disarming simplicity and inimitable charm.

**3. Allegro assai**   A brilliant, energetic and restless rondo. Despite certain chromatic passages, the thematic material displays none of the dramatic qualities of the first movement. This does not mean, however, that it is in any way frivolous. There is constant animation throughout the movement and a mood of shy, reticent gaiety.

# 19

## 1785 | Concerto for piano and orchestra in C Major, No. 21, K. 467

1. **Allegro maestoso**
2. **Andante in F Major**
3. **Allegro vivace assai**

Mozart continued his feverish activity. On March 9th, he finished writing the Concerto in C Major, K. 467, a work which seems almost staid after the tumult of the Concerto in D Minor. Three days later he gave it its first public performance, in the Mehlgrube theatre.

Leopold wrote to Nannerl:

"We never get to bed before one o'clock and I never get up before nine. We lunch at two or half past. The weather is horrible. Every day there are concerts; and the whole time is given up to teaching, music, composing and so forth. I feel rather out of it all. If only the concerts were over! It is impossible for me to describe the rush

131

*Mozart wearing the Order of the Golden Spur.*
*Copy of an unsigned portrait in oils. About 1777.*

and bustle. Since my arrival your brother's fortepiano has been taken at least a dozen times to the theatre or to some other house. He has had a large fortepiano pedal made, which stands under the instrument and is about two feet longer and extremely heavy. It is taken to the Mehlgrube every Friday and has also been taken to Count Zichy's and to Prince Kaunitz's."

Leopold described his son's fine apartment and the details of his daily life. He mentioned the exact "take" at each of the concerts, but he never breathed a word about the fact that Wolfgang had him, Leopold Mozart, enter a Freemason's Lodge.

In March Mozart was elevated from the degree of Entered Apprentice to that of Fellow Craft. In April he became a Master Mason.

It was spring. Mozart's second season in Vienna was coming to an end. He had every reason to be inordinately proud of his triumphs both as a pianist and as a composer, but he remained modest and friendly, always ready to meet music-lovers and to play for anyone who showed any taste for or knowledge of music.

For example, he never used his title of Knight of the Golden Spur, which Pope Clement XIV conferred on him in Rome in 1770. Gluck, on the other hand, had no hesitation in using his all the time. Indeed, Mozart only mentioned it once, in a letter from Mannheim to his father on November 22, 1777, which he signed: ". . . Wolfgang Amade Mozart, Knight of the Golden Spur and, as soon as I marry, of the Double Horn, Member of the Grand

Academies of Verona, Bologna. Oui, mon ami!"

\* \* \*

**1. Allegro maestoso** The first subject is a march in military time. Its rhythm dominates the entire movement. The horns and trumpets voice a plaintive appeal which is answered by the flute and oboes. The piano seems reluctant to make its appearance, but as soon as it does, it engages in an uninterrupted dialogue with the *tutti*. During the exposition, the piano introduces a second theme in G Minor, which anticipates the pulsing rhythm of the first movement of Mozart's Symphony No. 40, K. 550. The grandiose development reaches its point of culmination at Bar 253, where for one throbbing moment the listener's pleasure becomes almost unbearable. During the recapitulation, the plaintive appeal of the horns and trumpets is taken up again in melancholy fashion by the piano before the final virtuoso passages. The martial theme from the start of the movement also reaches its peak during the final portion of this majestic *allegro* which is one of the most complex and original in all of Mozart's piano concertos.

**2. Andante in F Major** This rustic nocturne is a triptych. During the first episode, the first violins sing a cantilena of indescribable tenderness over the triplets of the muted second violins and violas, and the pizzicatos of the double-basses. In the second episode, the piano repeats this heart-rending melody against the unobtrusive background of the strings; pungent chords, faintly dissonant, burst out in *sforzando* passages among the woodwinds. The movement ends with the full orchestra in action. The orchestration, entirely in filtered tints, displays a superb degree of refinement.

**3. Allegro vivace assai**   After the poignant beauty of the slow movement, this final piece of mischief could appear to be almsot irreverent were it not so delightfully witty. Although it would appear that Mozart was in a hurry to have done with it, it is drawn to its rapid conclusion by a master's hand.

**Works written between March 9th and July, 1785**

*Oratorio 'Davidde penitente', K. 469*
*Lied 'Gesellenreise', K. 468*
*Cantata 'Die Maurerfreude', K. 471*
*Lieder:*
    *— 'Der Zauberer', K. 472*
    *— 'Die Zufriedenheit', K. 473*
    *— 'Die betrogene Welt', K. 474*
*Fantasia for piano in C Minor, K. 475*
*Lied 'Das Veilchen', K. 476*

# 20

# 1785

# 'Maurerische Trauermusik', K. 477 (Masonic Funeral music)

Mozart was commissioned by the Vienna Musical Society to write an oratorio for Lent, 1785.

Since Vienna had not yet heard his Mass in C Minor, which had been sung only once in Salzburg two years earlier, he decided to adapt the 'Kyrie' and the 'Gloria' from that Mass to an Italian text which was probably furnished by the Abbé Lorenzo da Ponte, the Court poet. He composed two new arias for Valentin Adamberger and Caterina Cavalieri (Belmonte and Constanze in 'The Abduction from the Seraglio') and the trick was complete. The oratorio, 'Davidde penitente', K. 469 was performed on March 13th.

On April 24th, Mozart conducted his cantata 'Die Maurerfreude' ('Masonic Joy'), K. 471, at a banquet held in the lodge of 'The New-Crowned Hope'.

The next day, he and Constanze saw Leopold off on his way back to Salzburg. Neither father nor son had any way of knowing they were embracing for the last time.

Anton Klein, a poet whom Mozart met in Mannheim in 1778, sent him a libretto for an opera, 'Rudolf von Habsburg'. In a letter written on May 21st, Mozart told Klein he had not yet had time to look properly at the work, although this may very well have been just an excuse to avoid giving Klein an outright refusal.

In the spring of 1785, Mozart began to take an interest in Beaumarchais' 'Marriage of Figaro'. There were already several German translations of this work, but Mozart knew French fairly well and he preferred the original text.

He asked Lorenzo da Ponte to write him a libretto for a German opera based on Beaumarchais' work. Da Ponte wrote in his 'Memoirs':

"I liked the suggestion very much, and promised him to write one."

As is well known, Beaumarchais' comedy caused a considerable scandal in Paris when it was first performed. There were stormy demonstrations at every performance, the author was arrested, and so on. This helps to explain da Ponte's next sentence . . . "But there was a very great difficulty to overcome. A few days previous, the Emperor had forbidden the company at the German Theatre to perform that comedy, which was too licentiously written, he thought, for a self-respecting audience."

Nevertheless, Mozart and his librettist set to work. They were confident they could get the opera accepted by the emperor when the time came.

Unfortunately, da Ponte's knowledge of German was inadequate to allow him to write a libretto in that language. Mozart was bitterly disappointed, but he refused categorically to change his librettist. As a result, he had to agree to an *opera buffa*.

Rumours were circulating that the German National Theatre in Vienna was about to reopen its doors but, unfortunatelly, these proved to be quite untrue. This led Mozart to observe ironically in his letter to Anton Klein dated May 21st:

"Were there but one good patriot in charge — things would take a different turn. But then, perhaps, the German national theatre which is sprouting so vigorously would actually begin to flower; and of course that would be an everlasting blot on Germany, if we Germans were seriously to begin to think as Germans, to act as Germans, to speak German and, Heaven help us, to sing in German! !"

On June 8th, Mozart wrote a lied on one of Goethe's poems: 'Das Veilchen', ('The Violet'), K. 476. He gave it a sentimental little ending of his own invention. This is, incidentally, the one and only point of contact in music between the great poet and the 'little man with the wig and sword' who made such an impression on Goethe in Frankfurt in 1763.

During the month of July, Mozart wrote the 'Masonic Funeral Music', K. 477. The circumstances of its composition are unknown.

\*   \*   \*

This elegiac adagio in C Minor, 69 bars long, is full of Masonic symbolism. Well-marked rhythms, rests, parallel thirds and sixths, three flats to the key, are some examples. (Similarly, 'The Magic Flute' contains many examples of the symbolic use of the figure 3: three Ladies, three Genii, three temples, three ordeals, etc.) The work is set out as a solemn march, built around a Gregorian *cantus firmus* (beginning at the twenty-fifth bar) which Mozart noted on a separate sheet to make sure he would not lose sight of it, and which ends with a reassuring chord in C Major, symbolizing the victory of Light over Darkness.

The orchestra is made up of two oboes, a clarinets, three basset horns, a double-bassoon, two horns and the strings. The use of the lower register of the woodwinds gives this work a rich, sombre colour appropriate to a piece of funeral music. The two higher-pitched basset horns and the double-basson were added by Mozart after this work had been completed.

'Thamos, König in Aegypten', ('Thamos, King of Egypt') K. 345, on which Mozart worked in 1773 and 1779, included elements of a Masonic style. Mozart carries them further here and improved them even more in his cantatas of 1791, as well as in 'The Magic Flute', his Masonic masterpiece.

Between the composition of the 'Masonic Funeral Music' in July 1785 and that of the Quartet for piano and strings in G Minor, K. 478, completed on October 16th of the same year, Mozart's only work was a cantata for Nancy Storace, which is no longer extant.

# 21

## 1785 | Quartet for piano, violin, viola and violoncello in G Minor, K. 478

1. Allegro
2. Andante in B Flat Major
3. Allegro in G Major

By September, 1785, Mozart was nearly finished composing 'The Marriage of Figaro'. Lorenzo da Ponte knew there was a shortage of new operas for the theatre, so he took the opportunity to discuss 'Figaro' with Joseph II. The Emperor began by objecting that although Mozart was a wonder at instrumental music, he had written so far only one opera, 'The Abduction from the Seraglio', and nothing remarkable at that. Besides, this 'Marriage of Figaro', he had just forbidden the German troupe to use it!

"Yes, Sire", rejoined da Ponte, "but I was writing an opera, and not a comedy. I had to omit many scenes and

*Lorenzo da Ponte. Engraving*
*by Pekenino, after Rogers.*

to cut others quite considerably. I have omitted or cut anything that might offend good taste or public decency at a performance over which the Sovereign Majesty might preside. The music, I may add, as far as I may judge of it, seems to me marvelously beautiful."

"Good!" replied Joseph, "If that be the case, I will rely on your good taste as to the music and on your wisdom as to the morality. Send the score to the copyist."

Encouraged by Joseph's promise to allow the opera to be staged, Mozart threw himself into his work with re-doubled energy. But he could never allow himself to be completely monopolized by a single work, however important it might be, and on October 16th he set his opera aside briefly in order to create a new musical form — the quartet for piano and strings.

Mozart had signed a contract with the publisher Franz Anton Hoffmeister to write three such quartets. The first of the series, the Quartet in G Minor, is a gloomy work and difficult to perform. The public was cool toward it from the start. As a result, Hoffmeister asked Mozart not to send him the other two quartets.

However, a second was completed in 1786, shortly after the performances of 'The Marriage of Figaro'. This was the Quartet in E Flat Major, K. 493. It was equally as beautiful as the first and scarcely a whit less difficult to perform. But this time Artaria was the publisher.

The piano part, in the Quartet in G Minor, requires a virtuoso of the class of those who are capable of playing the most difficult piano concertos.

\* \* \*

**1. Allegro** The listener is struck immediately by the lack of repose and the severity of this movement. (Mozart himself must have found it sad and disturbing because he abandoned the key of G Minor in favour of G Major for the finale.) Piano and strings jointly state an energetic first theme, which is investigated at length. The second subject is marked in 4/4 time, but it suggests a 5/4 rhythm. One cannot fail to notice this odd effect. At times, the emphasis and scope of this movement give it the character of a piano concerto. When the second subject reappears, this time in the minor key, it intensifies the sense of despair induced by the movement as a whole.

**2. Andante in B Flat Major** As a contrast to the turbulence of the *allegro,* Mozart offers the lyrical beauty and peaceful tenderness of this eloquent *andante.* No storm threatens to mar its cool limpidity.

**3. Allegro in G Major** Here is a rondo of most curious construction. After stating the second theme, which is serious and solemn, Mozart departs from the accepted rules for rondos and instead of repeating the first theme, he proposes a third subject, then a fourth, and even a fifth. The Quartet in G Minor is one of his most richly melodic works. The elegance of the finale reminds us that it is contemporary with 'the Marriage of Figaro'.

*Quartet for piano, violin, viola, and violoncello in G Minor, K. 478*

**Works writen between October 16th and December 16th, 1785**

*Vocal Quartet 'Dite almeno', K. 479*
*Vocal Trio 'Mandina amabile', K. 480*
*Sonata for piano and violin in E Flat Major, K. 481*

# 22

## 1785 Concerto for piano and orchestra in E Flat Major, No. 22, K. 482

1. Allegro
2. Andante in C Minor
3. Allegro; andantino cantabile in A Flat Major

The concert season of 1784-85 brought Mozart great artistic success and plenty of money. However, money seemed to burn his fingers. He spent without reckoning and he gave countless dinners and receptions so that when autumn came he found himself in an embarrassing financial situation. It was then that he wrote the first of a long series of letters, each more distressing than the last, in which he tried to borrow money from various friends. This was to be the pattern over the last six years of his life.

The first of these letters, dated November 20th, was to his publisher, Franz Anton Hoffmeister, who sent him two ducats the same day.

On December 16th, Mozart completed the first of the three piano concertos he had planned for his next season, 1785-86: The Concerto in E Flat, No. 22, K. 482.

The Viennese continued to make much of the virtuoso and his concertos. On December 23rd, they turned out in great numbers for the first public performance of his new concerto and insisted on encoring the slow movement, the *andante* with variations. Mozart described this incident as "odd". He was no doubt surprised to find that this sweetly sad piece in C Minor could move to such a point the elegant public who attended his 'academien'. After daring to produce his Concerto in D Minor the previous season, Mozart doubless felt it wiser not to ask too much from the frivolous Viennese. This time he offered them a sparkling piece of work, totally devoid of all elements of distress.

His third Concerto in E Flat Major (No. 9, K. 271, and No. 14, K. 449, are also in this key) allows us to admire what a refined artist Mozart had become in the realms of expression and writing. In this concerto, and for the first time in a piano concerto, Mozart substituted oboes with clarinets.

**1. Allegro** This is one of the most grandiose first movements in all of Mozart's piano concertos. It begins with one of those demands for attention which are so common in Mozart's 'concertante' works (and which might be likened to the three raps in French theatres which signal the opening of the play). There is an abundance of thematic material, all of which is graceful, peaceful, energetic and majestic. The orchestration is exceptionally rich in texture.

**2. Andante in C Minor**  The theme of this aria with five variations and coda is, at the outset of the movement, stated by the muted strings alone. It is infinitely beautiful and at the same time sad, almost pleading. Mozart then shows us various aspects of this theme, rather like a playwright developing a character for the stage. The first variation consists of a somewhat ornate repetition of the theme by the soloist accompanied by the strings. The second is a little serenade in E Flat Major for wind instuments in which the clarinets have an important part to play. In the third variation, piano and strings give free rein to several impassioned effusions. The fourth, in C Major, consists of a joyful dialogue between the flute and the bassoon. In the fifth, we return to C Minor. The orchestra asserts itself and seems to show anger with a series of disquieting trills from the strings. In the coda, everything clears up again. It is easy enough to understand how that first-night audience in Vienna were so moved by the grace, radiant beauty and sheer eloquence of the movement as to require Mozart to repeat it for them.

**3. Allegro; andantino cantabile in A Flat Major**  This rondo in 6/8 time is a piece of hunt music complete with gallopings and horn-calls. The movement comes suddenly to a halt and Mozart sketches for us a delightful pastoral scene, an *andantino cantabile,* to which the voices of the clarinets and the bassoons lend a plaintive touch. The rondo then takes over once again and the movement comes to an end in a mood of unbridled joy.

**Works written between December 16th, 1785
and March 2nd, 1786**

*Rondo for piano in D Major, K. 485*
*Song with chorus 'Zerfliesset heut', K. 483*
*Chorus 'Ihr unsre neuen Leiter', K. 484*
*Adagio for two basset horns and bassoon in F Major,
K. 410*
*Adagio for two clarinets, two basset horns and bass clari-
net, in B Flat Major, K. 411*
*'Der Schauspieldirektor', K. 486*

# 23

**1786** Concerto for piano and orchestra in A Major, No. 23, K. 488

1. Allegro
2. Adagio in F Sharp Minor
3. Allegro assai

In December 1785, the Emperor Joseph II decreed that Vienna's eight Masonic Lodges be combined into two. From then on, Mozart found himself a member of the lodge of 'The New-Crowned Hope'; the Worshipful Master was Baron Tobias von Gebler, the author of 'Thamos, König in Aegypten', for which Mozart had written incidental music in 1773 and 1779.

For the inauguration of his new lodge, Mozart wrote a *lied* with chorus, K. 483, and a chorus, K. 484, as well as two *adagios* for wood-winds, K. 410 and K. 411. These four pieces were the last of his Masonic compositions until the year 1791.

151

On February 7th, 1786, the singspiel 'Der Schauspiel-direktor' ('The Impresario') was presented at the Schön-brunn palace. Joseph II had commissioned the text from Stephanie the Younger, the librettist of 'The Abduction from the Seraglio' and the music from Mozart to celebrate the arrival in Vienna of his brother-in-law, Albert of Saxe-Teschen, Governor of the Netherlands.

Mozart's contribution amounted to a witty overture in D major and four numbers for Valentin Adamberger, Caterina Cavalieri and Aloysia Lange. This was the first time that Aloysia had a part in one of her brother-in-law's artistic creations.

On March 2nd, Mozart finished work on his twenty-third piano concerto, the Concerto in A Major, K. 488. This is one of the two most popular and frequently played of all his piano concertos; the other being the Concerto in D Minor, K. 466.

\* \* \*

**1. Allegro** During the symphonic prelude, Mozart shows us all the thematic material for this movement, which is of much simpler construction than the *allegro* in his previous Concerto in E Flat Major, K. 482. The need for virtuoso display is also less apparent here, although this in no way means that the soloist is kept any less busy. The scoring is clear and simple; the style is both elegant and punctilious. There are no trumpets or kettledrums in the orchestra with the result that the resonance is less sparkling than in the twenty-second Concerto. Though they may seem similar,

Mozart's piano concertos are markedly different from each other in terms of their humour, colouring and the atmosphere they create.

**2. Adagio in F Sharp Minor**   Mozart wrote *adagio* on the score, but what emerges here is quite clearly an *andante*. (In a letter to his father dated June 9th, 1784, he stated firmly that there were to be no *adagios* in his concertos, only *andantes*.) This movement is an exquisite sicilienne. Written in the rare key of F Sharp Minor, it contains a central episode in which the woodwinds produce enchanting pastoral sounds. This meditative piece of music, so delicately coloured, is an example of classical perfection, clarity and conciseness. As in the first movement, Mozart's mood alternates between joy and sadness; we see him 'smiling through his tears'.

**3. Allegro assai**   Certain editions carry the marking of *presto* at the beginning of this rondo, which is one of the most staggering ever written by Mozart. The piano goes at a furious pace and there is a ceaseless flood of gay melodies and unexpected modulations. The absolutely irresistible charm of this movement alone is enough to justify the popularity of this concerto.

**Works written between March 2nd and March 24th, 1786**

*Duet 'Spiegarti non poss'io', K. 489*
*Scena 'Non piu tutto ascoltai', K. 490*

# 24

**1786** | Concerto for piano and orchestra in C Minor, No. 24, K. 491

1. Allegro
2. Larghetto in E Flat Major
3. Allegretto

For a single performance of 'Idomeneo' given by several vocalist friends of Prince Karl Auersperg, Mozart composed two new pieces on March 10th: the duet for soprano and tenor 'Spiegarti non poss'io', K. 489, to be sung by Mme de Pufendorf and Baron Pulini; and a *scena con rondo* for tenor, comprising the recitative 'Non piu tutto ascoltai' followed by the aria 'Non temer, amato bene' K. 490, with a violin obbligato intended for one of his close friends, Count August von Hatzfeld. (Within the year, Mozart was to suffer the grievous loss of this friend, who died of tuberculosis at the age of 31.)

Idamante's aria 'Non temer, amato bene' was written down as though it were a soprano part, either because Mozart still remembered the castrato who had sung the part in 1781, or else because he was thinking of having it sung by his lovely friend Nancy Storace. (It was only a few months after this that he composed the dramatic scene for soprano with piano obbligato 'Ch'io mi scordi di te?', K. 505, for her, using the same words as in Idamante's aria.)

At this time, Mozart also put the finishing touches to 'The Marriage of Figaro', which was planned for production at the end of April. It was Carnival time and he loved to dance; he went to a fancy-dress ball disguised as a Zoroastrian.

On March 24th, he wrote his twenty-fourth concerto, the Piano Concerto in C Minor, K. 491. If the Concerto in D Minor had revealed a much-troubled mind, his new concerto bore all the marks of utter despair.

One wonders what the first listeners must have thought on April 7th, when they heard Mozart play this work, since it is totally devoid of the usual prettiness of galant music.

They were probably incapable of grasping the profound beauty of the work; doubtless all they noticed was its length and its complexity. It must have bored them and it is quite possible that it was because of it that the Viennese began to lose interest in Mozart and his piano concertos.

His Concerto in C Minor is enough, of itself, to destroy the myth of 'the divine Mozart', the eternal child, the graceful Dresden porcelain figurine clad in a lace jabot and powdered wig. It is a virile, profound work of great sensitivity, the work of a man of thirty who has attained full maturity.

Here, Mozart assembles the largest orchestra he has yet used. It includes a flute, two oboes and two clarinets, two bassoons, two horns, two trumpets, a pair of kettledrums and the string. In the first movement he uses to great advantage the lower register of the strings and divides the violas.

\* \* \*

**1. Allegro**   The initial theme of this *allegro* bears a resemblance (although it is far more disturbing) to the first subject of the opening movement of the Concerto in E Flat Major, No. 14, K. 449, also in ¾ time. The piece overflows with passion and incessant chromatic effects which intensify its desolate sadness. Despite the second subject, which is more tender in mood, the character of the movement remains passionate throughout and its pulsing rhythm is always feverish. A series of major dramatic climaxes is followed by a coda which is surprisingly short. Exhaustion seems to overcome the orchestra and the piece ends *pianissimo*.

**2. Larghetto in E Flat Major**   In this rondo, we have the love scene from a great classical tragedy. The rondo-theme, which sets out an idea of exquisite simplicity, is followed by two episodes, more animated in nature, and during which the piano converses with the woodwinds. Both episodes are intensely emotional, particularly the second one, in A Flat Major, with its series of voluptuous thirds. The trumpets remain silent throughout the whole of this movement.

**3. Allegretto**  We resume the key of C Minor and, once again, the mood becomes charged with drama. It remains so, unrelentingly, to the end of this theme with eight variations even though two of them are relatively peaceful in nature (No. 4 in A Flat Major and No. 6 in C Major). From the beginning of the seventh variation, at Bar 200, the movement gives way to grief. Fierce passion rumbles unceasingly beneath the surface, bursting out into the open here and there, then subsiding. After the cadenza, the rhythm changes from 4/4 to 6/8, the feverish mood grows stronger and the movement comes to an end on a note of intense despair.

# 25

## 1786 'Le Nozze di Figaro', K. 492 ('The Marriage of Figaro')

On April 18th, Leopold Mozart informed his daughter that the first performance of 'The Marriage of Figaro' had been set for the 28th of the month. "It will be surprising if it is a success, for I know that very powerful cabals have ranged themselves against your brother. Salieri and all his supporters will again try to move heaven and earth to down his opera. Herr & Mme Duschek told me recently that it is on account of the very great reputation which your brother's exceptional talent and ability have won for him that so many people are plotting against him."

Just as with 'The Abduction from the Seraglio', there were indeed powerful factions opposed to Mozart. These were led by Salieri and Righini, the poet Casti, who was Lorenzo da Ponte's rival, and Count Rosenberg, the administrator of the theatre itself; all of them wanted to stop the new opera from being staged.

*Silhouettes of Stefano Mandini, Count Almaviva in*
*'The Marriage of Figaro'; Luisa Laschi, the Countess;*
*Sardi Bussani, Cherubino; Nancy Storace, Susanna;*
*and Michael Kelly, Basilio and Don Curzio.*

Salieri and Righini each had an opera ready to be produced; they were trying to have these put on before 'The Marriage of Figaro'.

Mozart swore he would burn his score rather than let himself be supplanted. Rumours were rife that even some of the singers in Mozart's own company were involved in these plots, with the exception of Nancy Storace and Michael Kelly, of course, who were personal friends of the composer.

Fortunately, Joseph II gave instructions to begin rehearsals and it seemed certain that the performances of 'Figaro' would indeed take place.

Count Rosenberg was furious and he raised all sorts of difficulties. On the pretext that ballets were forbiden in *opera buffa,* he tried to suppress the fandango in the third act. It took an order from the Emperor to have it reinstated.

The cast was brilliant. It included the best Italian opera singers in Vienna, with Luisa Laschi as Countess Almaviva, Stefano Mandini as the Count, Nancy Storace as Susanna, Francesco Benucci as Figaro, Sardi Bussani as Cherubino, Michael Kelly as Basilio and Don Curzio and, finally, Marianne Gottlieb (the future Pamina in 'The Magic Flute') as Barbarina.

"I remember at the first rehearsal of the full band", Michael Kelly tells us in his *Reminiscences,* "Mozart was on the stage with his crimson pelisse and gold-laced cocked hat, giving the time of the music to the orchestra. Figaro's song, 'Non pui andrai', Benucci gave with the greatest animation and power of voice. I was standing close to Mozart who, *sotto voce*, was repeating, 'Bravo! Bravo! Benucci'; and when Benucci came to the fine passage, *Cherubino, alla vittoria, alla gloria militar,* which he gave out with stentorian lungs, the effect was electricity itself. All the performers on the stage, and those in the orchestra, as if one person, shouted with a feeling of delight, vociferated 'Bravo! Bravo! Maestro! Viva, viva grande Mozart!' "

The first performance finally took place on May 1st, 1786, at the Burgtheater before the Emperor and his Court. All of Mozart's friends were among the audience, of course. Kelly reports that at the end of opera, he thought the audience would never stop applauding and calling for Mozart. Nearly every number was encored, which made the performance run twice as long as had been expected, so much so that the Emperor gave instructions that there were to be no encores at the second performance. Never hah an opera had a more complete triumph than Mozart's 'Marriage of Figaro'.

The Emperor's instructions were not obeyed. At the second performance, five numbers were encored and at the third, seven, not counting the duettino 'Aprite, presto aprite', which was repeated no less than three times.

Despite these initial successes (partly due to Mozart's Viennese friends and admirers), the fact remains that there were only nine performance of 'The Marriage of Figaro' in Vienna in 1786, which is not many. On December 18th, a new opera by Martin y Soler. 'Una Cosa rara', followed

'The Marriage of Figaro' at the Burgtheater and nothing more was heard of Mozart's latest opera until the twelve performances given in the autumn of 1789.

During the remainder of Mozart's lifetime, the work was sung a total of eighteen times, fifteen times in 1790 and three times in 1791.

Apparently, 'The Marriage of Figaro' displeased Joseph II and the Viennese even more than 'The Abduction from the Seraglio' because of the complexity of the plot and the startling novelty of the music, which proved too much for them. Its critics claimed it was too long and too difficult to sing. They did not like, moreover, the vulgar allusions to 'le droit de cuissage' and the servants who always seemed more clever than their masters.

Only in Prague at the end of this same year (1786) did 'The Marriage of Figaro' win its first genuine success and become unreservedly admired.

\* \* \*

Beaumarchais' original plan had been to make 'The Marriage of Figaro' a comedy interlaced with ariettas. In fact, his work lends itself admirably to being set to music. The main cuts made by da Ponte and Mozart included: in the third act, the important scene between the Count and Figaro, Marcellina's feminist demands and the trial scene, as well as, in the fifth act, Figaro's lengthy monologue.

The 'Marriage of Figaro' consists of an overture in D

Major (written two days before the opening performance), fourteen arias shared among the nine principal characters, six duets, two trios, a sextet, two choruses and the finales of the second, third and fourth acts. It may be fairly described as an 'opera of ensembles'.

Figaro has the largest number of solos. He asserts his character from the moment he sings the mocking, sarcastic cavatina 'Se vuol ballare' (No. 3). This scene does not appear in Beaumarchais' text, but it captures the spirit of the other monologues of Figaro, who despises his master and calls him 'contino' (the little Count). The valet demands equality and justice. Certainly, many Viennese must have been shocked by his provocative attitude and his claims to independence.

Figaro's second solo, 'Non piu andrai' (No. 9) replaces the conventional finale of the first act. This satirical military march produces an irresistible effect: it is the most popular number in the whole opera. Soon, Mozart was to hear it danced to in the taverns of Prague.

Figaro's third song, 'Tutto e disposto' (No.26) expresses his anguish at having been deceived by Susanna. Insulting to women though it may be, this aria reminds one that drama is at the source of this comedy.

Susanna is the busiest character in the opera. Her two arias are: 'Venite, inginocchiatevi' (No. 12) in the second act, a tender mocking aria which shows that she is by no means insensitive to Cherubino's charms during the naughty little game in which she undresses the page and then dresses him up again to the great amusement of the Countess; and 'Deh vieni, non tardar' (No. 27) in the fourth act, in which she sings of her love for Figaro even as she pretends to be waiting for the Count. Although she has only two solos, Susanna takes part in all the ensembles: the six duets, the two trios, the sextet and the three finales.

The Countess also has two arias: the cavatina 'Porgi, amor' (No. 10) — the perfect expression of love betrayed; and 'Dove sono' (No. 19) in which she mourns her happiness in days gone by, now lost forever.

The Count has only one aria: 'Hai gia vinta la causa' (No. 17) but it is very grand. It is the opera's second song of vengeance, the first being 'La Vendetta' (No. 4) sung by Bartolo. For a proper appreciation of Count Almaviva's character, it is very important to listen to him proclaiming that he cannot stand his servant's happiness and that it makes him suffer to see a man of Figaro's class winning the love of a woman whom he himself has been wooing in vain.

Cherubino is without doubt one of the most human and appealing characters in the opera. His first aria, 'Non so piu cosa son' (No. 6) expresses the emotions of a young, stammering boy who is beginning to be troubled by women and by the stirrings of love. Cherubino is no longer a child; if he were, neither the Count nor Figaro would be jealous of him. In 'La Mère coupable', the third part of Beaumarchais' Spanish trilogy, Cherubino is killed on the battlefield, after having fathered a child by Countess Almaviva. Had he not died, he would probably have become a sort of Don Juan.

Cherubino's arietta, 'Voi che sapete' (No. 11) joins Figaro's 'Non piu andrai' as one of the most effective numbers in the opera. In it, the page confesses his love for the Countess in scarcely veiled terms.

Bartolo, Marcellina, Basilio and Barbarina each sing an aria, but they contribute nothing to the plot.

Marcellina's 'Il capro e la capretta' (No. 24) and Basilio's 'In quegli anni' (No. 25) are usually omitted, but Bartolo's 'La Vendetta' (No. 4) is always retained. It is a rousing piece, in the purest style of *opera buffa*.

As for the cavatina 'L'ho perduta, me meschina' (No. 23) sung by Barbarina, who has lost the pin the Count instructed her to give to Susanna, it is one of the most dramatic moments of the whole opera. This sad little song in F Minor, created entirely by da Ponte and Mozart, expresses the simplicity of the disconsolate little errand-girl, the only pure and honest character in the opera.

The six duets are worthy of note. Susanna and Figaro sing the first two right at the beginning: 'Cinque . . . dieci' (No. 1) and 'Se a caso madama' (No. 2). Later 'Via resti servita' (No. 5) pits the two rivals for Figaro's affections (Susanna and Marcellina) against each other with incomparable humour, Mozart succeeds in capturing the exact tones of two women arguing. 'Aprite, presto aprite' (No. 14) is a masterpiece of conciseness, mischievousness and wit. 'Crudel! perche finora' (No. 16) shows Susanna flirting outrageouly with her master, who can hardly believe his own good fortune. Finally, the 'letter' song, 'Sull'aria' (No. 20) between the Countess and Susanna, is a charming duet, smoth-flowing and endowed with an unparallelled elegance.

The first of the two trios, 'Cosa sento' (No. 7) expresses Susanna's anger at the idea of Basilio's discovering the Count and Cherubino in her room. The terzetto 'Susanno, or via sortita' (No. 13) in the second act, depicts the Count's fury and the Countess' emotion in the scene where Cherubino jumps from the balcony.

The sextet 'Riconosci in questo amplesso' (No. 18) was Mozart's own favourite piece of the opera. This scene, in which Figaro realizes Marcellina and Bartolo are his mother and father, is the most comic in the entire production; its 'sua madre' and 'suo padre' are absolutely irresistible.

In the first act, the chorus sings 'Giovanni liete' (No. 8) during which the peasants arrive to thank the Count for having abolished 'le droit du seigneur'. In the third act, it also sings 'Ricevete, o padroncina' (No. 21), a chorus of homage from the peasant women to the Countess.

The finale of the second act, like those of the third and fourth acts, is a proper little opera in miniature. It consists of six movements on stage with eight characters taking part. The finale of the third act, with chorus, is in four parts: Figaro's wedding march; the *allegretto* of the young peasant girls; Susanna's fandango; and the Count's invitation to the wedding celebrations.

The finale of the fourth act, in which eleven characters take part, is divided into six movements: the play between Cherubino and the Countess disguised as Susanna; the play between the Count and his wife disguised as Susanna; the play between Figaro and Susanna disguised as the Countess; explanations between Figaro and Susanna; discovery of the hoax and, finally, the scene in which the Count makes his apologies to his wife, who accepts them resignedly. Each section of this finale carries a specific indication of the required tempo: *andante, con un poco di moto, larghetto, allegro molto, andante* and *allegro assai.*

In these elaborate ensemble movements, many ideas are expressed with extreme rapidity. Mozart uses these movements to show the artistry with which he can have several characters speak at the same time. The movements are extremely complex. In his 'Memoirs', da Ponte points out that while they must be closely associated to the action, they must also admit of a new twist in the plot and be of special interest: they offer a perfect opportunity for the singers to show off their individual talents and for the composer to assert his genius.

**Works written after the production of 'The Marriage of Figaro' up to August 1st, 1786**

*Quartet for piano and strings in E Flat Major, K. 493*
*Rondo for piano in F Major, K. 494*
*Horn Concerto in E Flat Major, No. 4, K. 495*
*Trio for piano, violin and violoncello in G Major, K. 496*
*Twelve duos for basset horns, K. 487*
*Four Notturnos for three voices, K. 436, K. 437, K. 438 and K. 439*

# 26

## 1786 | Piano Sonata for four hands in F Major, K. 497

1. Adagio; allegro
2. Andante in B Flat Major
3. Allegro

Shortly after the production of 'The Marriage of Figaro', Pasquale Bondini, Director of the Prague Opera, visited Mozart to negotiate the rights for the Prague performances of his opera.

The "take" from 'Figaro' had been good, but it hardly left Mozart any better off. He still had debts and he was paying a high rent for his apartment. His future was as uncertain as ever. Constanze was expecting a child in October. Because it was summer-time, it was quite impossible to give any further concerts. Mozart had to revert to teaching.

Among his pupils there was one of whom he was particularly fond: Thomas Attwood, a 21 year-old English composer. Attwood tells us that Mozart would sometimes propose a game of billiards instead of a lesson and that as they played he would expound his aesthetic principles to his pupil.

In the summer of 1786 Mozart took a new student to live with him as a paying guest. The eight-year-old boy, Johann Nepomuk Hummel, was to be a future friend of Beethoven. The child adored Mozart and stayed with him for two years. One evening three years later, when Hummel was giving a concert in Berlin, he was told that Mozart was in the theatre. The boy rushed immediately to his former master and showered him with all the signs of his deepest affection.

Mozart also gave lessons to Franziska, the sister of his friend Baron Gottfried von Jacquin. Both brother and sister were numbered among Mozart's most cultured friends and they frequently invited him to their house to attend their musical evenings every Wednesday. Mozart felt happy in these surroundings where he was received with respect. He enjoyed being understood and appreciated for his true worth.

Since early childhood, Mozart had an almost pathological need for tenderness and friendship. When growing public indifference, poverty and illness began slowly to drive him into solitude, his pain was aggravated by the suffering he felt at being deprived of the affection of a large circle of friends.

Mozart never forgot the friendly instruction he received

from Johann Christian Bach in London, when he was struggling to write his first symphonies at the age of eight. The announcement of Bach's death in 1782 deeply saddened him.

"I suppose you have heard that the English Bach is dead? What a loss to the musical world!"

As a final tribute, he used a theme by Johann Christian at the beginning of the *andante* movement of his Piano concerto in A Major, No. 12, K. 414.

In 1770, during his first tour of Italy, Mozart met Thomas Linley in Nardini's house, in Florence. The young English violinist was the same age as Mozart. Their friendship was short but warm and spontaneous, and the two boys wept when the time came for them to part. Later Mozart made another friend, in Bologna — the Czech composer Josef Mysliwecek, whom the Italians called affectionately 'il divino Boemo'.

The gay, candidly erotic letters (many of which were well spiked with scatalogic references) Mozart wrote Maria Anna Thekla, his young cousin from Augsburg (also known as 'The Basle') are filled with mischievousness and love. Maria Anna was the one Mozart begged to return to Salzburg with him in Jannuary 1779 when he had to reassume the yoke of Colloredo.

Despite the bitterness he experienced during his lifetime at being continually torn from the places and people he loved most, this remarkable man made — and lost — many outstanding friends.

Finally, one of the main reasons Mozart became a Freemason had to do with his need for friendship and fraternal association. He had many Masonic friends, among whom he included Anton Stadler, Emmanuel Schikaneder and Michael Puchberg. After Mozart's death, Puchberg became the tutor to Mozart's sons.

Mozart wrote masterpieces for his friends. The Trio for piano, violin and violoncello in E Major, K. 542, and the Divertimento for string trio in E Flat Major, K. 563, were both dedicated to Michael Puchberg. He also dedicated several magnificent arias to Gottfried von Jacquin who had a fine bass voice. In 'Mentre ti lascio', K. 513, one can almost *feel* the warmth of the friendship between the two men.

When the opportunity arose, Mozart consented to pay a little attention to a fellow Salzburger, the horn-player Ignaz Leutgeb (or Leitgeb) who kept a cheesemonger's shop in Vienna. Although he found it hard to take the fellow seriously, and he always poked fun at him as the price of his friendship, Mozart wrote four concertos for horn and orchestra for him.

He embellished the rondo of the first, the Concerto in D Major, K. 412, with ridiculous exclamations: "Adagio" — a lei Signor Asino — animo — presto — idiot! — da bravo — corragio — bestia — bravo poveretto — respira un poco! — avanti! questo poi va al meglio — ah! trillo de pecore — grazie al Ciel! basta, basta!"

On the second, the Concerto in E Flat Major, K. 417, he wrote, "Wolfgang Amadeus Mozart has taken pity on Leutgeb, donkey, ox and fool — Vienna, May 27th 1783"

The fourth, the Concerto in E Flat Major, K. 495, which was completed on June 26, 1786, is written in blue, green, red and black inks. Apparently, anything to do with poor Leutgeb drove Mozart to friendly leg-pulling, but the four concertos he wrote for him are very fine, especially the fourth, in which the slow movement is a most expressive *romanze.*

Thus, this summer of 1786, one of the happiest of his life, Mozart divided his time between the Jacquins and his friends Thomas Attwood, Nancy and Stephen Storace and Michael Kelly.

Mozart finished the Sonata in A Major, K. 497, on August 1st, so he could play it with his pupil Franziska von Jacquin. This sonata is fully worthy of inclusion among his masterpieces of chamber music, and is the most noteworthy of the seven piano compositions he wrote for four hands — the friendly genre *par excellence.*

He wrote a second sonata for Franziska in May 1787, the Sonata in C Major, K. 521. It is a brilliant piece of music, rather difficult (in Mozart's own words) but less personal.

\* \* \*

**1. Adagio; allegro**  Preceded by a slow introduction, the *allegro* assumes proportions that are almost symphonic. In this piece, Mozart arranges, stylistically, a happy marriage between the galant and the learned to the entire satisfaction of scholars and amateurs alike.

**2. Andante in B Flat Major**  This noble and solemn piece

resembles a grand love-duet from an *opera seria*. A sonata for four hands has the advantage (compared with a solo sonata) of a fuller, richer resonance and is also able to indulge in some marvellous imitation.

**3. Allegro** This brilliant finale contains several themes, some mischievous and capricious, others pleasant and sensual. Mozart exploits them all in a rather whimsical fashion. The two pianists must keep their minds on their performances at all times, for the piece is full of unexpected technical traps.

# 27

## 1786

# Trio for piano, clarinet, and viola in E Flat Major, K. 498

1. **Andante**
2. **Minuet; trio in G Minor**
3. **Allegretto**

On August 5th, four days after he finished the Piano Sonata for four hands in F Major for Franziska von Jacquin, Mozart dedicated a new work to her, the Trio for piano, clarinet and viola in E Flat Major, K. 498.

Legend has that this trio was written in the Jacquin's garden, during a game of skittles. Indeed, it could very well have been in these very circumstances that Mozart sketched the basic outline for the composition of this masterly piece. What is really astonishing is that he could conceive two works as different as the Sonata for four hands and this Trio at one and the same time. And that he could write them with only four days between them!

On August 19th, just two weeks later, Mozart wrote yet another magnificent work, the String Quartet in D Major, K. 499.

Earlier, we cited the year 1784 as an example of a highly productive period in Mozart's life. 1786 was even more productive.

The tally runs as follows:

| | |
|---|---|
| January 10th: | Rondo for piano in D Major, K. 485 |
| January 14th: | Song with chorus 'Zerfliesset heut', K. 483 |
| January 14th: | Chorus 'Ihr unsre neuen Leiter' K. 484 |
| February 3rd: | 'Der Schauspieldirektor', K. 486 |
| March 2nd: | Piano Concerto in A Major, No. 23, K. 488 |
| March 10th: | Two pieces for a repeat performance of 'Idomeneo', K. 489 and K. 490 |
| March 24th: | Piano Concerto in C Minor, No. 24, K. 491 |
| May 1st: | 'The Marriage of Figaro', K. 492 (date of first performance) |
| June 3rd: | Quartet for piano and strings in E Flat Major, K. 493 |
| June 10th: | Rondo for piano in F Major, K. 494 |
| June 26th: | Horn Concerto in E Flat Major, No. 4, K. 495 |
| July 8th: | Trio for piano, violin and violoncello in G Major, K. 496 |

| July 27th: | 12 Duos for basset horns, K. 487 |
| August 1st: | Piano Sonata for four hands in F Major, K. 497 |
| August 5th: | Trio for piano, clarinet and viola in E Flat Major, K. 498 |
| August 19th: | String Quartet in D Major, K. 499 ('Hoffmeister') |
| September 12th: | Piano Variations in B Flat Major, K. 500 |
| November 4th: | Andante with five variations for piano four hands in G Major, K. 501 |
| November 18th: | Trio for piano, violin and violoncello in B Flat Major, K. 502 |
| December 4th: | Piano Concerto in C Major, No. 25, K. 503 |
| December 6th: | Symphony in D Major, No. 38, K. 504 ('Prague') |
| December 26th: | 'Ch'io mi scordi di te?', K. 505 |

The Trio in E Flat Major was first performed at one of the Jacquin's Wednesday musical parties featuring Fräulein von Jacquin at the piano, Mozart himself on the viola and the clarinettist Anton Stadler.

Since his discovery of the clarinet in London in 1764, Mozart had had a fondness for this versatile and expressive instrument whose voice is so much warmer than the somewhat sour oboe. He composed three masterpieces for the clarinet: the Trio in E Flat Major, K. 498; the Quintet in A Major, K. 581; and the Concerto in A Major, K. 622. It should be remembered, however, that at the time Mozart composed his 'Skittles' Trio, the clarinet was still a new instrument with few devotees. Therefore, when Artaria published it he thought it prudent to title it as follows: *'Trio per il Clavicembalo o Forte Piano con l'accompagnamento d'un Violino e Viola. La parte del Violino si puo eseguire anche con un Clarinetto'.*

But Mozart was quite definitely thinking of a clarinet — and not a violin — when he composed this trio. The clarinet and the viola add an unaccustomed range of colour to this original work. Although the brilliant voice of the clarinet is never allowed to overbear the thinner tones of the stringed instrument, the viola nonetheless plays a subordinate role to its companion throughout the three movements.

Mozart conceived the three parts of this trio with exceptional restraint, much as though he was striving to express only the most intimate and tender sentiments in this happy work.

With respect to the form of the piece, the 'Skittles' Trio introduces two new features: firstly, an *andante* instead of an opening *allegro;* and secondly, a minuet instead of a slow movement.

* * *

**1. Andante** This movement in 6/8 time presents an affirmative opening subject, embellished with a graceful, insistent *grupetto* and a secondary theme which, although more lyrical, is not markedly different from the first. It is a delicately structured movement in sonata-form, easy-flowing and clearly written throughout. The resonant tone of the clarinet endows it with a note of poignancy.

**2. Minuet; trio in G Minor**   The pleasant, robust minuet encompasses a trio to which the triplets of the viola impart an agitated rhythm. The coda combines elements of the minuet and of the trio.

**3. Allegretto**   In the second episode of this final rondo (very much in the style of a concerto) the triplets from the trio in the previous movement reappear, first with the violin then with the clarinet (using the lower register, the chalumeau). This episode in C Minor is the most fully-developed of the entire piece. The second episode in a rondo more or less takes the place of the normal development in a sonata movement.   In the third episode, Mozart repeats (this time without the syncopation) the second subject of the initial *allegro* of the Quartet for piano and strings in G Minor, K. 478. To end the movement, he presents a new and joyful version of the rondo-theme.

# 28
## 1786 | String Quartet in D Major, K. 499 ('Hoffmeister')

1. Allegretto
2. Minuet; trio in D Minor
3. Adagio in G Major
4. Allegro

On August 8th, 1786, Mozart wrote a certain Sebastian Winter, a valet and musician attached to the Court of the Prince of Fürstenberg at Donaueschingen. (Winter had been the Mozarts' friseur in Paris in 1764.) Mozart wanted to negotiate the sale of several of his works.

"If His Highness should so desire, I shall send him in future all the new works which I compose. Further, I venture to make a little musical proposal to his Highness which I beg you, my friend, to put before him. As His Highness possesses an orchestra, he might like to have works composed by me *for performance solely at his court,* a thing which in my humble opinion would be very gratifying."

Mozart included a list of his recent composition in his letter, which he ended with the following words:

"I do trust that His Highness will not take my proposal amiss, if it does not suit him, for it is indeed prompted by an impulse of genuine anxiety to serve His Highness diligently, which in such a situation as mine is only possible if one can be sure of at least some support and can afford to give up less important tasks."

On September 30th, Mozart sent three symphonies and three concertos to the Prince of Fürstenberg with an explanatory note to Sebastian Winter on how to transpose the clarinet parts in the Concerto in A Major, K. 488, should these instruments not be available in Donaueschingen.

No profitable arrangement resulted from this approach by Mozart. He received 143 florins in payment for the copies of his scores. He was never heard to speak of Sebastian Winter again.

On August 19th, he completed the imposing String Quartet in D Major for the publisher Hoffmeister (probably to pay off some debt or other).

Mozart had certainly made a name for himself in Vienna by then, partly as a performer of his own piano concertos, but mainly as the composer of 'The Abduction from the Seraglio', the only one of his five major operas really to achieve success during his lifetime. But despite this, he had not managed to assure himself a "fixed yearly salary" which would enable him to "work with greater peace of mind". In fact, he never managed to do it.

The Haydn Quartets and 'The Marriage of Figaro' added nothing to his glory, On the contrary, his reputation as a piano virtuoso began to be overshadowed by his reputation as a 'difficult' composer who wrote not for the public at large but for a small circle of connoisseurs.

No one knew better than Mozart himself that his star was on the wane. Had he not predicted in June 1781 that the Viennese were a volatile people, fickle in their affections and that one day they would tire of him too? His prediction was coming true. But he had also prophesied that he would become rich in the meantime. Unfortunately, that was far from being the case in August 1786.

Except for the 'Hoffmeister' Quartet, Mozart's string quartets were actually planned as a series: the three Divertimentos of 1772; the six Milanese Quartets of 1772-1773; the six Viennese Quartets of 1773; and the six Haydn Quartets. Later, in 1789 and 1790, he would compose the three Prussian Quartets, forming part of a series of six commissioned by Friedrich Wilhelm II of Prussia. Mozart's death prevented the completion of this series.

1. Allegretto   The first movement is built almost entirely around a march theme which is stated at the beginning by the quartet playing in unison. This theme is made up of two short rhythmic motifs which lend themselves admirably to contrapuntal play. A second, more emphatic subject, and then a third suggesting the use of triplets, are heard only during he exposition, and the recapitulation. (Meanwhile, the idea of triplets has been put forward and will be taken up by Mozart in due course.) The develop-

ment, rich in ingenious modulations, concerns itself only with the initial march theme, which Mozart plays with in a charmingly light-hearted fashion. The entire movement is a close-knit unit of perfection.

**2. Minuet; trio in D Minor**  In the elegant, vigorous minuet, the four instruments are given parts to play which are surprisingly independent of each other. The scoring of the trio is neat and delicately executed. Quivering triplets couvert this trio (long before Mendelssohn and Berlioz) into a proper little Queen Mab Scherzo.

**3. Adagio in G Major**  The four instruments converse intimately among themselves, although the general tone is one of detachment. Only the first violin experiences occasional moments of exaltation. The entire movement is punctuated by imperious accents. As in the *allegretto,* Mozart's main interest in this *adagio* is centred on the first, firmly stated subject.

**4. Allegro**  Here, the triplets reappear to form a fragmentary theme which is interrupted twice by a full bar of silence. Mozart then contrasts this theme with the second subject (Bars 44 to 59) during the development section. There is nothing gay or amusing in this music, which tends to justify Mozart's reputation as a 'difficult' composer. The listener is greeted with bold and somewhat baffling harmonies, and strict counterpoint. Yet, Mozart displays consumate skill in the finale as he darts continuously to and fro, playing with the idea of the triplets which he first put forward in the *allegretto* and from which he now exploits all the possibilities.

## Works written after August 19th to December 4th, 1786

*Variations for piano in B Flat Major, K. 500*
*Andante for piano four hands in G Major, K. 501*
*Trio for piano, violin and violoncello in B Flat Major,*
*K. 502*

# 29

## 1786 | Concerto for piano and orchestra in C Major, No. 25, K. 503

1. **Allegro maestoso**
2. **Andante in F Major**
3. **Allegretto**

On October 18th, while Mozart was discussing the possibility of a long trip to England with his English friends, Constanze gave birth to a son, whom they named Johann Thomas Leopold.

It was out of the question to leave the mother alone in Vienna with her new-born baby and his brother Karl, who was now two years old. It was equally out of the question to take the children to England with them.

Mozart learned that his father was looking after Nannerl's son at his home in Salzburg. He wrote and asked him if he would also look after their children for a while, since he had plenty of domestic help.

On November 17th, Leopold wrote to his daughter:

"I had to reply today to a letter from your brother, and this took me a considerable time. So I cannot write very much to you. Moreover it is late and I want to go to the play today, as I have a free pass, and have only just finished that letter to Vienna. You can easily imagine that I had to express myself very emphatically, as your brother actually suggested that I should take charge of his two children, because he was proposing to undertake a journey through Germany to England in the middle of next carnival... Not at all a bad arrangement! They could go off and travel — they might even die — or remain in England — and I should have to run off after them with the children. As for the payment which he offers me for the children and for maids to look after them, well — Basta! If he cares to do so, he will find my excuse very clear and instructive."

On the very day Leopold sent off his letter of refusal, Mozart, in Vienna, buried his little Johann Thomas, who had died two days before. The child was scarcely one month old. Mozart's grief is easy to discern from the solemn tone of two works which he finished one after the other at the beginning of December: the Piano Concerto in C Major, No. 25, K. 503 on the 4th, and the Symphony in D Major, No. 38, K. 504 on the 6th.

On December 18th, the ninth and last performance of 'The Marriage of Figaro' was given in Vienna. Not until July 1789 would this work be sung there again.

Martin y Soler's opera 'Una Cosa rara' was the production which followed at the Burgtheater; it was an immense success. (Before long, Mozart borrowed a motif from this opera and gave it to the orchestra which played at Don Giovanni's supper.)

Around Christmastime he received an invitation from Count Thun, together with a letter written collectively by the musicians of Prague, urging him to come to that city to direct a performance of his 'Figaro'.

\* \* \*

**1. Allegro maestoso** The movement opens with a series of majestic chords. It is the most grandiose exposition in all of Mozart's piano concertos. A rhythmic motif soon emerges from the thematic material which spreads slowly through the whole movement giving it its heroic character. It is made up of the four notes from the 'Destiny' theme of Beethoven's Fifth Symphony.

**2. Andante in F Major** The solemn grandeur of the first movement gives way to the dignified reserve of a magnificent duet between the piano and the wood-winds, against an unobtrusive accompaniment from the strings. Mozart wrote this _andante_ in the same vein as Susanna's song in the garden: 'Deh vieni, non tardar', which is also an _andante_ in F Major.

**3. Allegretto** The graceful and charming theme of this rondo retains some of the traits of the march-theme from the first movement, although here it is stripped of its imposing character. During the second episode, after having stated an energetic theme in A minor, Mozart strikes three orchestral chords and then offers us a new

189

*Constanze Mozart.*
*Miniature painted in*
*Vienna in 1783.*

melody in F major which is staggering in its expressiveness, yet at the same time so simple it requires a true Mozartian to savour its full beauty.

# 30

## 1786   'Ch'io mi scordi di te?', K. 505

On December 26th, Mozart entered a new work in his thematic catalogue: the dramatic scene and rondo for soprano, with piano obbligato and orchestra, 'Ch'io mi scordi di te?'. He added the note, "für Madselle Storace und mich".

In this song of farewell, written for Nancy Storace just prior to her return to England, Mozart expressed without restraint his tender feelings for the girl who had made such a ravishing Susanna in 'The Marriage of Figaro', and his sadness at having her leave without him.

He took care to include a piano part (which he himself would play) which underlined and punctuated the highly significant words of the rondo: "Fear naught, dearest love, my heart is thine forever".

Nancy Storace and Mozart had known each other since the days of the first Haydn Quartets. They had weathered the anti - 'Figaro' intrigues together and with Michael Kelly, Nancy had supported Mozart throughout this time of crisis. They had planned to tour Italy, Germany and England together — a beautiful dream which would never come true. The ties of friendship between them were very strong.

*Silhouette of Mozart*
*cut by*
*Löschenkohl,*
*in 1786.*

'Ch'io mi scordi di te?' conceals nothing of Mozart's feeling for the girl. Miss Storace's voice and Mozart's piano can be heard exchanging promises of eternal love. The recitative is full of passion, the rondo overflows with tenderness and emotion. Yet we know nothing of the singer's feeling for Mozart. The letters which she must have written to the composer from England have disappeared. It is easy to assume that she admired Mozart the artist, but what did she think of Mozart the man — the man whose many portraits (most of them false) provide only a confused and contradictory image?

Mozart was not a man of strong constitution. His head was on the large side, his nose was strong, his eyes blue and his hands small and plump. "He was a remarkably small man", writes Michael Kelly in his "Reminiscences", "very thin and pale, with a profusion of fine fair hair, of which he was rather vain ... He was kind-hearted, and always ready to oblige; but so very particular, when he played, that if the slightest noise were made, he instantly left off ..."

\* \* \*

The orchestra which accompanies this dramatic scene is made up, in addition to the necessary piano, of two clarinets, two bassoons, two horns and the strings. The words of the recitative are by an unknown author —probably Mozart himself. The words of the rondo are signed by the Abbé Varesco and had previously been used in the tenor's song. 'Non temer, amato bene', K. 490, composed nine months earlier for a revival of 'Idomeneo'. This aria, which included a violin solo to be played by Mozart's friend Count von Hatzfeld, is quite beautiful although it did not possess the warmth and force of expression which transform the musical tribute to Nancy Storace into a masterpiece.

\* \* \*

1. **Recitative: 'Ch'io mi scordi di te?'**   The opening words are an unhappy cry of protest from the heroine: "How should I forget thee, love?" Then she sings, "Should Death o'ertake me, I would stand my ground and wait upon Him. But that I should cherish some other face, give some other man my love — that were unthinkable indeed! O, I should die for grief." These words, sung in G Minor, bring the recitative to a close. In two bars, Mozart changes the key to E Flat Major and introduces the rondo.

2. **Rondo in E Flat Major:**   **'Non temer, amato bene'** This begins with an *andante,* built in the A-B-A rondo form. The rondo proper is marked *allegretto* and comprises a subject, three episodes (the second of which, in C Minor, forms the section of the development) and a coda. The sheer beauty of the dialogue which takes place between voice and piano from the *andante* onward turns this composition into a masterpiece absolutely unique in the story of Mozart's works. Besides, where in the whole body of written music can one find promises of love expressed so forcefully?

196

# 31
# Symphony in D Major, No. 38, K. 504 ('Prague')

1786

1. **Adagio; allegro**
2. **Andante in G Major**
3. **Presto**

On January 9th, 1787, Mozart set out for Prague accompanied by Cosntanze and his future brother-in-law, the violinist Franz de Paula Hofer, who was to marry Josepha Weber the following summer.

This was the first of Mozart's three trips to Prague, a city where he had been unreservedly admired since the performances of 'The Abduction from the Seraglio' in 1782. It is easy to understand the nature of the welcome the people of Prague, oppressed as they were by the Emperor of Austria, prepared for 'Figaro', the opera of liberty!

Count Johann Thun, a great admirer of Mozart and a fellow Mason, welcomed the travellers into his home and supervised the installation of a piano in the composer's room. He organized chamber music sessions for Mozart's sake and took him to the theatre to hear 'Le Gare generose' by his friend Paisiello.

Mozart was delighted to see Franz and Josepha Duschek again; they had been his friends for the past ten years. After the strain of the last few months he managed to relax in this warm atmosphere in which he felt himself surrounded by love and admiration.

He wrote to Gottfried von Jacquin and told him that at one particular ball he had watched the guests dance to the music of his opera, arranged as German dances.

"For here", he wrote, "they talk about nothing but 'Figaro'. Nothing is played, sung or whistled but 'Figaro'. No opera is drawing like 'Figaro'. Nothing, nothing but 'Figaro'. Certainly a great honour for me!" Clearly, the Prague audiences were not finding 'Figaro' too long or too difficult!

On January 14th, Mozart and Hofer attended a performance of the opera. The composer was greeted with thunderous applause when he entered the hall.

On the 19th there was a concert at which Mozart conducted his Symphony in D Major which he had completed only on December 6th, 1786. This concert scored a success the like of which had never before been seen in Prague. When it ended, Mozart had to improvise on the piano for a full half-hour. Each time he attempted to leave the stage, the audience insisted he return.

Suddenly, from the back of the hall, someone called out 'Figaro!' Mozart gave a lengthy improvision on the song 'Non piu andrai'. The entire audience went wild with excitement and gave him an ovation which it seemed would never stop.

Symphony in D Major, No. 38, K. 504
('Prague')

The next day, Mozart directed a triumphant performance of 'The Marriage of Figaro'.

His successes in Prague were among the most magnificent of his career. As a result, the name of this friendly city continues to be associated with the Symphony in D Major.

\* \* \*

Not since the Symphony in C Major, written in Linz in 1783, had Mozart tackled the symphonic form. His Symphony in D Major is known as the 'Symphony without a minuet', although it was not the first time that Mozart had dispensed with the minuet in a symphony. His Symphonies in B Flat Major, No. 33, K. 319; in C Major, No. 34, K. 338, and the 'Linz' Symphony, No. 36, K. 425 do not contain minuets.

The Symphony in D Major is scored for an orchestra without clarinets, but with trumpets which give it a brilliant resonance.

\* \* \*

1. **Adagio; allegro** A majestic, disquieting preamble precedes an *allegro* which is at the same time both joyful and melancholy. The development is the most meticulously worked out of all the first movements of Mozart's symphonies. A recently discovered sketch shows how carefully he elaborated the numerous motifs which go into the working of his contrapuntal scheme.

**2. Andante in G Major**   At the beginning of this movement, a subtle and poetic song is heard. The second subject is a rhythmic figure which seems somewhat unimpressive to begin with, but which soon assumes an important role. the listener must have a sharp ear to recognize it; in the able appearance of this piece, although it never bursts out forcefully. The mood is one of sweet sadness and lofty sentiments.

**3. Presto**   To please 'Figaro's' admirers in Prague, Mozart draws the principal theme of his finale from the *duettino* of Susanna and Cherubino: "Aprite, presto aprite". However, the listener must have a sharp ear to recognize it; in the opera this motif, which serves as an introduction to the duet, is played very rapidly. The movement is one of classic rigour; it is vigorous and it displays a frank good humour.

**Works written between December 26th, 1786 and May 16th, 1787**

*6 German Dances for orchestra, K. 509*
*Rondo for piano in A Minor, K. 511*
*Aria 'Alcandro lo confesso', K. 512*
*Aria 'Mentre ti lascio', K. 513*
*Rondo for horn and orchestra in D Major, K. 514*
*String Quintet in C Minor, K. 406*
*String Quintet in C Major, K. 515*

# 32

## 1787 | String Quintet in G Minor, K. 516

1. **Allegro**
2. **Minuet; trio in G Major**
3. **Adagio ma non troppo in E Flat Major**
4. **Adagio in G Minor; allegro in G Major**

Mozart indulged himself to his heart's content in Prague, surrounded by the admiration of the general public and comforted by the love of his friends. He wrote six German Dances, K. 509, for a ball, using a full orchestra for the first time in his dance music — piccolo, flutes, oboes, clarinets, bassoons, horns, trumpets, kettledrums and strings without violas, as was customary. Despite the honours which were heaped on him in Prague, Mozart longed to return to Vienna. His successes in Prague brought him not only a pleasant amount of money, but also a commission from Bondini (the director of the company which had performed 'The Marriage of Figaro') for a new Italian opera on any subject he chose. He would be paid his fee as soon as the score was finished. He was also to receive an allowance to cover his travelling and accommodation expenses when he returned to Prague for rehearsals at the end of the year.

On February 10th, Mozart was back in Vienna with Constanze. He was stunned to learn of the sudden death, in Bonn, of his dear friend Count August von Hatzfeld. Not long after, he said his sad farewells to Thomas Attwood and Stephen and Nancy Storace.

Michael Kelly departed as well: "I went to take leave of the immortal Mozart, and his charming wife and family . . . I could hardly tear myself away from him; and, at parting, we both shed tears."

On April 4th, with Constanze pregnant once again, Mozart received upsetting news from Salzburg: his father was seriously ill.

Mozart immediately wrote a letter full of resignation and hope — but one which also reveals profound anguish.

"This very moment I have received a piece of news which greatly distresses me, the more so as I gathered from your last letter that, thank God, you were very well indeed. But now I hear that you are really ill. I need hardly tell you how greatly I am longing to receive some reassuring news from yourself. And I still expect it; although I have now made a habit of being prepared in all affairs of life for the worst. As death, when we come to consider it closely, is the true goal of our existence, I have formed during the last few years such close relations with this best and truest friend of mankind, that his image is not only no longer terrifying to me, but is indeed very soothing and consoling! And I thank my God for graciously granting me the opportunity (you know what I mean) of learning that death is the *key* which unlocks the door to our true happiness. I never lie down at night without reflecting that — young as I am — I may not live to see another day. Yet no one of all my acquaintances could say that in company I am morose or disgruntled. For this blessing I daily thank my Creator and wish with all my heart that each one of my fellow-creatures could enjoy it . . . "

In the same letter, Mozart mentioned the sudden death of Count von Hatzfeld to his father. "He was just thirty-one, my own age. I do not feel sorry for him, but I pity most sincerely both myself and all who knew him as well as I did. I hope and trust that while I am writing this, you are feeling better. But if, contrary to all expectation, you are not recovering, I implore you by . . . not to hide it from me, but to tell me the whole truth or get someone to write it to me, so that as quickly as is humanly possible I may come to your arms. I entreat you by all that is sacred — to both of us. Nevertheless I trust that I shall soon have a reassuring letter from you; and cherishing this pleasant hope, I and my wife and our little Karl kiss your hands a thousand times and I am ever your most obedient son, W. A. Mozart."

In this spring of 1787, Mozart wrote two string quintets: one in C Major, K. 515; the other in G Minor, K. 516. The latter quintet reveals the anguish and the sadness Mozart felt at the departure of very dear friends, at his father's illness and at the death of Hatzfeld. It is one of his most revealing works.

The Mozarts moved house when they returned to Vienna from their visit to Salzburg at the end of 1783 after they learned of the death of their son Raimund Leopold. They did the same on thier return from Prague. They left their large apartment on the Landstrasse where little Johann Thomas had died only a few months before and moved into new quarters on the same street, only a few steps from the Jacquins' house. It was in this new apartment that Mozart finished the String Quintet in G Minor on May 16th.

Here, too, about the same time, he was visited by a young man (born sixteen years earlier in Bonn) who had come to Vienna to finish his musical studies: Ludwig van Beethoven.

Mozart has been accused of having received Beethoven with indifference. No doubt Mozart had little affection for child prodigies. He had suffered too much during his own childhood at having been one himself and he very likely distrusted this young Beethoven — people were saying far too many good things about him.

On the day of young Beethoven's visit, Mozart was in the company of some of his friends. So he took his visitor into a room nearby and listened to him play for a moment or two, without really giving him his full attention. Then Beethoven asked Mozart to give him a theme and proceeded without hesitation to improvise on it in such a remarkable fashion that Mozart hastened to say to his friends, "Keep your eyes on this boy. Some day he will give the world something to talk about".

Beethoven left Vienna at the beginning of July. He did not return until 1792, after Mozart's death.

It is not known for whom Mozart wrote the two string quintets in the spring of 1787, or why, at about the same time, he rearranged his poignant 1782 Serenade for wind instruments in C Minor as a string quintet. Perhaps he planned them for Friedrich Wilhelm II of Prussia, who was an amateur violoncellist, and for whom he was to compose three string quartets in 1789 and 1790.

On the other hand, it is known that his next two string quintets, the first in D Minor, K. 593 and the second in E Flat Major, K. 614, were commissioned by another amateur, the rich Hungarian merchant, Johann Tost.

\* \* \*

**1. Allegro**  This is a feverish movement. Its resonance is tragic; its rhythm is haunting. It is also extremely brilliant and lyrical. The feverish rhythm and intense expression of this *allegro* reminds the listener of the first movement of the great Symphony in G Minor.

**2. Minuet; trio in G Major**  A restless minuet, punctuated by *forte* accents which are like cries of anguish. The simple, pure beauty of the trio provides a brief moment of calm.

**3. Adagio ma non troppo in E Flat Major**  An admirable aria, heart-rending in tone and disturbing in rhythm. All five instruments are muted. The heavy atmosphere is sometimes almost suffocating.

*Ludwig van Beethoven, from the lithograph of a
silhouette by Joseph Neesen. About 1786.*

**4. Adagio in G Minor; allegro in G Major**   In the slow introduction the listener hears once again the drum-like rhythm which agitates the first three movements and which serves as the unifying element of the whole quintet. This preamble opens into an *allegro* designed (like so many finales in Mozart's tragic works) to sweep away sadness and gloomy thought. It is carefree without ever being frivolous. It dances along happily, although over the length of its course, its gaiety seems a little forced.

The seven string quintets left us by Mozart are all written for two violins, two violas and a violoncello.

**Works written between May 16th
and August 10th, 1787**

*Six lieder:*
   *'Die Alte', K. 517*
   *'Die Verschweigung', K. 518*
   *'Das Lied der Trennung', K. 519*
   *'Als Luise . . .', K. 520*
   *'Abendempfindung', K. 523*
   *'An Chloe', K. 524*
*Piano Sonata for four hands in C Major, K. 521*
*'A Musical Joke', K. 522*

# 33
# Serenade in G Major, 'Eine Kleine Nachtmusik', K. 525 ('A Little Night Music')

**1787**

1. Allegro
2. Romanze: andante in C Major
3. Minuet; trio in D Major
4. Allegro

On May 28th, after a brief illness, Leopold Mozart died at Salzburg. He was 68 years of age. Mozart's work and family obligations kept him in Vienna so he did not attend the funeral.

Father and son had loved each other dearly in former days. When he was a child, Mozart used to say that his father came immediately after God.

In later life, their relationship cooled considerably. There were arguments and occasional estrangements. Leopold disapproved of his son's behaviour and accused him of being unstable and frivolous. Wolfgang, for his part, longed to espace from his father's despotism. He left Colloredo despite Leopold's upbraidings and he married Constanze against his father's wishes. In the end, a deep rift developed between them.

After their father's death, Wolfgang and Nannerl came to a friendly arrangement over the inheritance. Nannerl sent Wolfgang all the scores which he had left in his father's house, together with some of Leopold's books. She received a final letter from her brother on August 2nd. 1788. After that, brother and sister lost touch with one another completely.

The day following his father's death, May 29th, Mozart wrote a note to Baron von Jacquin asking him to forward a piano sonata for four hands which he had just completed to his sister, Franziska. The note ended with this P.S. "I inform you that on returning home today I received the sad news of my most beloved father's death. You can imagine the state I am in."

After this brief funeral oration, Mozart lost no time getting back to the composition of his new opera for Prague, 'Don Giovanni'. If we can believe the librettist's *Memoirs,* the subject was submitted to Mozart by Lorenzo da Ponte himself. We know enough about Mozart, however, to speculate a little as to how intimate must have been the part he played in the elaboration of this tragicomic intrigue which is so rich in interesting human problems.

The month of July was devoted exclusively to the composition of the opera. During August, Mozart interrupted his work twice. First, on the 10th, in the middle of the second act of 'Don Giovanni', to write the Serenade for strings in G Major (which he himself christened 'Eine Kleine Nachtmusik'); and then on the 24th, to write the magnificent Sonata for violin and piano in A Major, K. 526.

The circumstances surrounding the composition of "A Little Night Music" are not known. What emerges here is not another string quintet like those Mozart wrote a few months earlier, but rather a proper serenade for two violins, a viola and a violoncello reinforced by a double-bass. The absence of wind instruments seems to indicate that the serenade was not intended to be played in the open air. On the other hand, it hardly seems likely that a work so perfectly put together was conceived as an accompaniment for some fashionable reception with guests talking and laughing, coming and going, eating and drinking. There can be no doubt, however, that it was so conceived, for it does not belong to the genre of chamber music. It is a true serenade which is both elegant and scholarly, with a little opening fanfare in the style of the Salzburg serenades. It has themes of popular appeal, it speaks in sensual, graceful tones; its movements are simple, short and concise.

Perhaps Mozart wrote it simply because the idea for it came into his head and its originality gripped his ima-

*Leopold Mozart. Unsigned portrait in oils. About 1780.*

gination as with the Serenade in C Minor. Or it may have come to him as he was composing 'Don Giovanni', in a moment of buoyant or intense happiness, or because he felt the need to relax — simply to give himself the pleasure of creating the most perfect, most joyful festive music.

In his thematic catalogue, Mozart wrote *"Eine Kleine Nacht Musick, bestehend in einem Allegro, Menuett und Trio. Romance. Menuett und Trio, und Finale"*. The first of the two minuets he mentions was torn from the original manuscrit score and has never been found.

**1. Allegro** This movement, characterized by its spontaneity and ingenuous charm, is in sonata form. The entire piece is carefully arranged and is filled with dignity and beauty.

**2. Romanze: andante in C Major** There is a kinship between this sweetly innocent *romanze* and Belmonte's romanze in 'The Abduction from the Seraglio': 'Wenn der Freude Trännen fliessen'. Here Mozart provides a dreamy interlude, interrupted by an episode in C Minor which seems to shiver in a frightened way, thereby breaking the serene mood for a moment or two.

**3. Minuet; trio in D Major** The minuet is a model of dignity and poise. The trio, written in supremely elegant fashion, is full of grace and dignity.

**4. Allegro** This rondo overflows with joy. It is difficult, once one has heard it, to forget its theme, a delightfully neat and fresh little Viennese song.

# 34

## 1787 | Sonata for violin and piano in A Major, K. 526

1. Allegro molto
2. Andante in D Major
3. Presto

Lorenzo da Ponte left a highly-coloured, certainly exaggerated account of how he set about writing the libretto of 'Don Giovanni'.

If we can believe the flamboyant Abbé, he worked on three librettos simultaneously: 'Axur, Re d'Ormuz' in the mornings, for Salieri (this work was based on Beaumarchais' 'Tarare'), 'L'Arbore di Diana' in the afternoons, for Martin y Soler (this was the best of the three and was probably his own original work), and, finally, 'Don Giovanni' in the evenings, for Mozart (after reading a few pages from Dante's 'Inferno').

Da Ponte would have us believe he was at his desk twelve hours a day, his Tokay, at his right hand and his Seville tobacco at his left. In front of him stood a bell with which he would summon his chambermaid, a charming young sixteen-year-old girl. He drank many a brimming glassful of strong wine every day, smoked pipe after pipe — and rang his bell "rather frequently" — so he wrote. After finishing 'Eine Kleine Nachtmusik', Mozart buried himself once more in 'Don Giovanni' for fourteen days — only to break off again on August 24th, this time to write the best of his sonatas for violin and piano, the Sonata in A Major, K. 526, which was to be his last work in this particular style. The Sonata in F Major, K. 547, which he wrote in 1788, is really a work of no importance which Mozart himself described in his thematic catalogue as a "piano sonatina for beginners, with a violin".

In his youth, Mozart composed over twenty sonatas for piano accompanied by violin. More often than not, however, these works could be played without violin accompaniment.

With the Sonata in C Major, K. 296, written for his pupil Therese Pierron-Serranius, in Mannheim in 1778, Mozart began to give the violin more freedom in his sonatas for piano and violin. In the Sonata in A Major, the violin becomes completely independent. There is no denying that this work blazed the trail for Beethoven's great sonatas for violin and piano.

\* \* \*

**1. Allegro molto**   This is an imposing movement in sonata-form, filled with *concertante* elements. Quite unceremoniously, it sets forth a theme with a nervous rhythm in 6/8

time and which is particularly ingenious in conception.
In the spirited development which follows, the three-part
counterpoint is learned without being in any way pre-
tentious. Again, Mozart achieves a happy fusion of the
old and the new in this composition: the rhythmic pulsing
beat is quite irresistible. In this work, Mozart seems to
have invented a new way of breathing. And also new
ways of thinking and of feeling, for this sonata offers a
perfect blend of vivacity and intelligence.

**2. Andante in D Major**   This is one of Mozart's most
original slow movements. Piano and violin combine at
the outset to state a mysterious theme, which sets an
atmosphere of spell-binding calm and induces a mood of
deep meditation. This music describes an inner vision
of almost unbearable beauty.

**3. Presto**   No less than the *allegro molto,* this impetuous
finale is a work of pure virtuosity, refined and witty, interspersed here and there with truly marvellous transports
of lyrical intensity.

# 35
# 1787 | 'Don Giovanni', K. 527

On September 3rd, Mozart was distressed to lose another friend — his doctor, Sigmund Barisani. As always, his grief was expressed in these terms: those who die are happy; the unhappy ones are those who survive them.

A few days later, he arrived in Prague with Constanze, who was then six months pregnant. His librettist, Lorenzo da Ponte, arrived shortly thereafter. All of them were housed in hotels facing each other on the same street. In fact, they were so close to each other that the two men could talk to one another through their open windows. Unfortunately, da Ponte had to leave Prague before the *première* of 'Don Giovanni'.

The opera Mozart brought with him to Prague was almost completed. Apart from the overture, only a few pieces had still to be written or modified. Mozart attended every rehearsal. He was an excellent producer and could be relied upon to get the best from the singers' on-stage movements.

"In the first place," he wrote to Gottfried von Jacquin, "the stage personnel here are not as smart as those in Vienna, when it comes to mastering an opera of this kind in a very short time. Secondly, I found on my arrival that so few preparations and arrangements had been made that it would have been absolutely impossible to produce it on the 14th, that is, yesterday."

The opening of 'Don Giovanni' had, in fact, been advertised for September 14th, to mark the arrival in Prague of the Archduchess Maria Theresa of Tuscany and her new husband, Prince Anton of Saxe. The management of the theatre had demanded a copy of the libretto from the authors in order to check it before the performance.

Perhaps Mozart and da Ponte were afraid of scandalizing Prague's distinguished guests of honour with a plot describing the adventures of a rake. While this hardly seems likely, they nonetheless submitted an incomplete libretto, and carried on about it to such an extent that in the end 'The Marriage of Figaro' was presented on September 14th instead.

Further delays were caused by the illness of one of the singers and also by several alterations which da Ponte made in the libretto at the request of the composer.

In Prague, the two men made the acquaintance of the famous Giovanni Casanova de Seingalt, who was at that time employed as a librarian by a wealthy Bohemian family. What an extraordinary meeting it must have been! Mozart, the immortal author of 'Don Giovanni'; Casanova, the Don Juan of his day; and the Abbé da

Ponte, who wrote his libretto in a haze of Tokay and in the arms of a sixteen-year-old chambermaid.

After the departure of his librettist, Mozart left his hotel (The Three Golden Lions) and went with Constanze to live with Franz and Josepha Duschek in their Villa Bertramka on the outskirts of Prague.

"I am far too much at the disposal of other people and far too little at my own" he complained in a letter to Jacquin.

Mozart usually took part in social events quite willingly, but he felt nervous on the eve of the presentation of 'Don Giovanni'. What would the good people of Prague, who had welcomed 'The Marriage of Figaro' so warmly, think of this new work, which was so different from the first? Besides, the libretto was far from perfect. There had not been time to work it out properly.

The traditional story has it that Mozart composed the overture to 'Don Giovanni' only two days before the *première* of the opera, with Constanze making him drink punch and keeping him awake with stories.

On November 3rd, the Prague 'Oberpostzeitung' carried a report that: 'Don Giovanni or The Stone Banquet', the long-awaited opera by the *maestro* Mozart, was performed on Monday, October 29th by the Italian Opera Company of Prague, under the direction of the composer; music-lovers everywhere were agreed that nothing like it had ever been seen in Prague before and that this extremely difficult work had been very well executed, in spite of the short time devoted to rehearsals.

'Don Giovanni' was written for the same company which previously performed 'The Marriage of Figaro' in Prague. Like the earlier opera, it contained three major female roles and two major male roles. The part of Don Giovanni was sung by Luigi Bassi, who was then 21 years old (and the darling of Prague). He had previously been Count Almaviva in 'Figaro'.

On the 4th of November, Mozart confirmed the success of his opera in a letter to Gottfried von Jacquin.

"My opera 'Don Giovanni' had its first performance on October 29th and was received with the greatest applause. It was performed yesterday for the fourth time, for my benefit . . How I wish that my good friends, particularly you and Bridi, were here just for one evening in order to share my pleasure! But perhaps my opera will be performed in Vienna after all! I hope so. People here are doing their best to persuade me to remain on for a couple of months and write another one. But I cannot accept this proposal, however flattering it may be."

\*   \*   \*

In his thematic catalogue, Mozart classifies 'Don Giovanni ossia il Dissoluto punito' as an *opera buffa*.

For the Viennese performances of this work in May 1788, Mozart cut the final sextet, thereby giving the work a tragic ending. He described it on the title-page of the libretto as a *dramma giocoso*.

Among Mozart's operas, 'Don Giovanni' stands out in that

the elements of tragedy and comedy in it are so inter-
mingled that one is never quite sure to which class it
belongs.

The most dramatic scene in the opera (and the one for
which Mozart wrote the most serious music) is the one in
which the hero takes supper with the statue of the Com-
mendatore. There is no denying that when the curtain
falls on this scene it produces a most gripping effect.
However, this was not Mozart's and da Ponte's original
intention; in the original version, 'Don Giovanni' had
a comic ending with a moral message, in the accepted
*opera buffa* tradition.

Once again, to please the public of Prague, Mozart and
da Ponte chose an extravagant and facetious comedy with
rough-hewen characters who are far less engaging than
those in 'The Marriage of Figaro'. What they offered the
good people of Prague, furthermore, was not a subtle
comedy with a complicated plot, but a spectacular show
— a true ancestor of the 'musical comedy' of our day —
filled with astonishing effects and just the thing to please
everybody.

As in 'The Mariage of Figaro', the hero of 'Don Giovanni'
is a cynical gentleman who is attended to by a cheeky manservant. However, there is a great difference between the
shrewd, sly Figaro and the lumpish Leporello. And the
punishment reserved for Almaviva is light indeed compared with what befalls Don Giovanni.

'Don Giovanni' has everything needed to please an audience: gaiety and gravity, humour and farce, debauchery

and religion — and let us not forget a class warfare even more bitter than that in 'Figaro'. In short, the formula could hardly fail.

At least ten of the twenty-four numbers in 'Don Giovanni' were bound to ensure the success of the opera:

1. 'Madamina' (No. 4), the famous catalogue aria in which Leporello brandishes shameful statistics under Donna Elvira's nose, with a derisive accompaniment from the orchestra.

2. The *duettino* 'La ci darem la mano' between Don Giovanni and Zerlina (No. 7), during the subtly sensual scene in which the young peasant girl is seduced.

3. Don Giovanni's aria 'Finch'han dal vino' (No. 11), which is notable for its energy and brevity.

4. Zerlina's aria 'Batti, batti, o bel Masetto' (No. 12), ironic but tender.

5. The finale of the first act (No. 13), with the three orchestras playing a minuet, a country dance and a German dance simultaneously, and the general atmosphere of elegant masquerade.

6. The *canzonetta* 'Deh vieni alla finestra' (No. 16), a delightful serenade accompanied by a mandolin and the strings.

7. The aria 'Vedrai, carino' (No. 18), during which Zerlina promises her husband Masetto the sweetest of remedies to cure him of his ills and, in somewhat forward fashion, makes him put a hand on her breast.

8. Ottavio's big aria 'Il mio tesoro' (No. 21), which gives

the one tenor in the cast his opportunity to display his talents.

9. The finale of the second act (No. 24), in which the listener hears three popular arias of the time, taken from the operas 'Una Cosa rara' by Martin y Soler, 'I Due Litiganti' by Sarti, and 'The Marriage of Figaro' by Mozart — this is, of course, 'Non piu andrai'.

10. Finally, the entire supper scene between Don Giovanni and the statue — a terrifying scene, with its three trombones, its orchestral effects and the hero's spectacular descent into the nether regions.

Nor should any of the following be overlooked: the overture in D Minor, sombre and menacing, but containing some comic elements as well; Elvira's outstanding aria 'Ah! fuggi il traditor!' (No. 8), with its angry tones which reflect the character so accurately; Anna's vows of vengeance 'Or sai, chi l'onore' (No. 10), preceded by important recitatives with orchestral accompaniment; the admirable mask trio (an *adagio* in B Flat Major) in the finale of the first act; the wicked Don Giovanni's aria 'Meta di voi qua vadano' (No. 17), underlined by sarcastic comments from the orchestra; and, finally, the magnificent sextet 'Sola, sola in bujo loco' (No. 19), which begins with a cry of distress from Elvira, who is terrified to find herself alone in the darkness.

Anna's great aria 'Non mi dir, bell'idol mio' (No. 23), preceded by the recitative 'Crudele? Ah no, mio bene!' aroused Berlioz' fury. In his 'Memoirs' he states that by writing this song Mozart was guilty of the most hateful crime that can be committed against good taste and common sense.

Actually, the piece begins by Donna Anna expressing her touching love for Don Ottavio, and then turns into a splendid piece of bravura designed solely to show off the singer's vocal technique. It is precisely because of these unfortunate flourishes that Berlioz could not forgive Mozart — a composer for whom he nevertheless had the highest admiration.

Like most composers of opera of his day, Mozart was expected to comply with certain customs and conventions. A romantic, free-thinking 19th-century composer like Berlioz was quite unable to admit that one could make concessions to theatrical realism for the purpose of pandering to the exhibitionistic tendencies of a *prima donna.*

In the 18th Century, everyone knew the story of the famous Spanish rake, and no one was in any danger of taking it seriously. How could anyone possibly be moved to pity by the fate of a hero who dines with a stone statue, and who disappears into the flames of Hell in mid-supper! And how could one resist bursting into laughter when the other characters in the play then begin to sing an uplifting little moral song for the edification of the audience!

Fundamentally, Don Giovanni is a tragic character, the slave of an inexorable passion which makes him desire every woman he sees. "You should know", he tells Leporello, "that I need them more than the food I eat or the air I breathe." However, his constant fear of being caught and the shame of his continual flights give him a comic aspect. To win Donna Elvira's lady's-maid, he goes to the ridiculous length of dressing up in his own manservant's clothes.

Don Giovanni is not the great tragic dreamer imagined by Cervantes; his cynicism is icy, his courage inescapable. But, like Don Quixote, he is accompanied by a buffoon whose cowardice serves to emphasize his master's courage — for Leporello is an essentially comic character (as, indeed, are Zerlina and Masetto).

Donna Anna is a sad — or perhaps long-suffering — character from an *opera seria,* even though she is made to take part in the comic sextet at the end of the opera. Donna Elvira is the major tragic figure of the opera. She is devoured by wrath and dreams only of revenge, yet she too finds herself frequently caught up in farcial situations. As, for example, when she is forced to listen to the catalogue of her unfaithful husband's amorous escapades, and later to undergo the horror of succumbing to Don Giovanni for a second time — only to discover that it is Leporello, clad in his master's clothing.

As for Don Ottavio — that boring, solemn puppet — his only *raison d'être* is to follow Donna Anna about like a faithful little lap-dog and sing his one big aria.

**Works written between October 29th, 1787
and January, 1788**

*Aria 'Bella mia fiamma', K. 528*
*Lieder:*
   *'Das Kleinen Friedrichs', K. 529*
   *'Das Traumbild', K. 530*
   *'Die kleine Spinnerin', K. 531*
*Vocal Trio 'Grazie agl'inganni tuoi', K. 532*

# 36
# Piano Sonata
# in F Major,
# K. 533

1788

1. **Allegro**
2. **Andante in B Flat Major**
3. **Rondo in F Major, K. 494 (1786)**

After the strain of writing 'Don Giovanni', Mozart was happy to take a few days' rest with the Duscheks at the Bertramka. One day, in an attempt to make him write an aria which he had promised her, and which he kept putting off, Josepha Duschek shut him up in a pavillon in the garden with pen, ink and paper. She would not let him out, she told him, until the aria was finished.

Mozart agreed — on one condition: he would not give her the aria unless she succeeded in singing it perfectly, at first sight.

Having struck that bargain, Mozart proceeded (for his own amusement) to make the aria as difficult as possible, putting in all sorts of unexpected modulations and strange intervals which would catch an unwary singer completely off her guard. We can only hope that poor Josepha passed the test with honours. In any case, as Karl Mozart recollects it, that is how Wolfgang Mozart came to write his second great song of farewell dedicated to a singer: 'Bella mia fiamma', K. 528.

The Mozarts left Prague in mid-November. In Vienna, Gluck had just died after an apoplectic stroke. Early in December, Joseph II appointed Mozart to the post previously held by his illustrious senior — that of chamber musician and composer to the Imperial and Royal Court. However, Mozart's salary was only 800 florins, instead of the 2000 which Gluck had received. Philosophically, he tried to console himself with the thought that at least no other chamber musician was getting as much.

His financial situation was so bad at this time that he had to give up his Landstrasse apartment and take more modest lodgings in a little street near the Graben. In these new quarters, on December 27th, Constanze gave birth to their fourth child, a daughter, Theresia. Karl, the only one of their three sons who had survived, was three years old.

In January, 1788, Mozart undertook to write a piano sonata for the publisher Franz Anton Hoffmeister, in payment for some debts he owed him. This was the Piano Sonata in F Major, K. 533. He wrote the first two movements, then, inexplicably, stopped work. To this day, no one knows why. At the time of publication, Mozart completed this unfinished sonata by adding a rondo he had composed in June 1786. However, this rondo has been reworked in such exquisite fashion that it is tempting to think that Mozart might perhaps have been so pleased with it that he wrote an *allegro* and an *andante* afterwards, to build his rondo into a sonata.

\* \* \*

**1. Allegro** Although this movement is solidly contrapuntal and written in a major key, it succeeds in arousing emotions and in expressing the deepest feelings. Instead of ending this *allegro* with a coda, Mozart prolongs the recapitulation and picks up again a theme which had appeared all by itself at the end of the exposition and remained until now unused. This conclusion produces a most vivid effect.

**2. Andante in B Flat Major** This slow and strangely beautiful movement grows ever more sombre after the double bar until it becomes downright severe. It contains an astonishing passage of harmonic progressions in sixths, thirds and sevenths, which is quite without parallel in any of Mozart's other works, and which blends into the context of the music in the most natural way. These first two sonata movements are written for a piano with a greater range than those used by Mozart heretofore.

**3. Rondo in F Major, K. 494** The modifications introduced by Mozart into this rondo of 1786 consist, first of all, of a marvellous three-part passage in F Minor, which gives weight to the piece. Next, the conclusion has been condensed into a contrapuntal cadenza calling for a lower register than that used in the first part of the rondo. In the last twelve bars, Mozart restates the rondo-theme one last time, in the lower register — thus giving it a

*Josepha Duschek.  Engraving
by Clar, after van Haake.*

new character, somewhat disturbing in nature and rather inconclusive.

**Works written from January up to June 22nd, 1788**

*Contredanse 'Donnerwetter' for orchestra, K. 534*
*Contredanse 'La Bataille' for orchestra, K. 535*
*Six German Dances for orchestra, K. 536*
*Piano Concerto in D Major, No. 26, K. 537 ('Coronation')*
*Aria for soprano 'Ah se in Ciel', K. 538*
*Aria for tenor 'Della sua pace', K. 540a*
*Duet 'Per queste tue', K. 540b*
*Aria 'Mi tradi quell'alma ingrata', K. 540c*
*Arietta for bass 'Un Bacio di mano', K. 541*

# 37
# Trio for piano, violin and violoncello in E Major, K. 542

1788

1. Allegro
2. Andante grazioso in A Major
3. Allegro

   In January 1788, in his capacity as the new composer to the Imperial and Royal Court, Mozart wrote some dance music, as his duties required. Since the Emperor was then at war with the Turks, Mozart christened one of his contredanses 'La Bataille', which seemed an apt title.

In February, Mozart wrote the Piano Concerto in D Major, No. 26, K. 537. His purpose in doing so is not known, particularly as the work does not seem to have been played in Vienna that season. He played it in Frankfurt in October 1790, on the occasion of the coronation of the future Emperor Leopold II, and because of this it has become known as the 'Coronation' Concerto.

Joseph II was intrigued by the tales he heard concerning the success of 'Don Giovanni' in Prague, and he gave instructions to have the opera performed in Vienna.

Rehearsals began in April. At the request of the tenor Francesco Morella, who was playing the role of Don Ottavio, Mozart agreed to replace 'Il mio tesoro' with a somewhat easier aria, 'Della sua pace'. He composed two other new pieces — a duet for Leporello and Zerlina, 'Per queste tue manine', which is usually omitted nowadays, and the aria 'Mi tradi quell'alma ingrate' for the new Donna Anna, who was the well-known singer, Caterina Cavalieri.

The Viennese production of 'Don Giovanni' opened on May 7th at the Burgtheater. However, the Emperor did not attend. The opera was sung fourteen times during the year. Da Ponte tells us that nobody seemed pleased with it. "Everyone, except Mozart, thought that there was something missing."

When he finally heard it, Joseph II said: "That opera is divine; I should even venture that it is more beautiful than *Figaro*. But such music is not meat for the teeth of my Viennese!"

"Give them time to chew on it!", replied Mozart. He could not accept the notions that his opera was melodically too complex to suit the current taste, and that it was, in general, too difficult for the singers, orchestra and audience.

In the end he came to say — not without bitterness — that he had written 'Don Giovanni' solely for the people of Prague, for himself and for his friends.

On June 17th, Mozart wrote to Michael Puchberg, a rich Viennese and a talented musician with whom Mozart had made chamber music on several occasions. Mozart asked him for a fairly large loan — one or two thousand florins — on which he offered to pay interest.

"You yourself will surely admit *the sense and truth* of my statement when I say that it is difficult, nay impossible, to live when one has to wait for various odd sums. If one has not at least *a minimum of capital* behind one, it is impossible to keep one's affairs in order. *Nothing* can be done with nothing."

If Puchberg would be good enough to lend him this money, Mozart explained, he would be able ". . . to work with a mind *more free* from care and *with a lighter heart,* and thus *earn more."* But he hastened to add — doubtless afraid of the possibility of a refusal — "If you should find it inconvenient to part with so large a sum at once, then I beg of you to lend me until tomorrow *at least a couple of hundred gulden,* for my landlord in the Landstrasse has been so importunate that in order to avoid an unpleasant incident I have had to pay him on the spot, and this has made things very awkward for me!"

The same day, the Mozarts moved into the Three Stars House at 135 Währingergasse, on the outskirts of Vienna. This was the most modest accomodation they had yet occupied since their marriage. Only a few years before, he had been one of the darlings of Vienna as a pianist and composer, supporting a large establishment in splendid quarters —

now he was reduced to this.
Mozart was forced to admit to himself, albeit bitterly, that in actual fact this particular move made no difference to him. Indeed, he almost welcomed it.

"As it is, I have very little to do in town and, as I am not exposed to so many visitors, I shall have more time for work. If I have to go to town on business, which will certainly not be very often, any fiacre will take me there for ten kreuzer."

At the end of his letter to his friend Puchberg, in which he apologized for being poor and out of favour, Mozart added this P.S. "When are we to have a little musical party at your house again? I have composed a new trio!"

He was referring to the Trio in E Major, which he completed five days after this letter (on which, incidentally, Michael Puchberg wrote: "Sent 200 florins").

At this point in his life, Mozart was no longer giving concerts. He was no longer invited into the elegant homes of the capital, as he had been in days gone by. Clearly, the Viennese were aware that he was hard up and crippled with debt. Perhaps the entire city already considered Mozart to be finished as a musician.

In his last letter to his sister, dated August 2nd, Mozart begged Nannerl to ask Michael Haydn to lend him some of his church music compositions.

"It is now exactly a year since I wrote to him and invited him to come and stay with me; but he has not replied . . . So I urge you to arrange this for me in the following way. Invite him to your house at St. Gilgen and play to him some of my latest compositions. I am sure he will like the Trio and the Quartet."

The quartet to which Mozart was referring is the second quartet for piano and strings, the Quartet in E Flat Major, K. 493; the trio is the Trio in E Major, K. 542. Mozart finished the trio on June 22nd, four days before the Symphony in E Flat Major, No. 39, K. 543.

Mozart was generally extremely conservative as far as tonalities were concerned, and he preferred to confine himself to simple keys. For example, when he took three fugues from Bach's 'Well-Tempered Clavier' in 1782, and transcribed them for string trio, he rejected the 'difficult' keys of D Sharp Minor, F Sharp Minor and F Sharp Major in favour of D Minor, G Minor and F Major.

The key of E Major is very rare in Mozart's music. We meet it in his operas (Sarastro's aria 'In diesen heil'gen Hallen' in 'The Magic Flute'; the cemetery scene in 'Don Giovanni'). But the Trio, K. 542, is his only instrumental work in E Major. This trio is the most beautiful of the six trios for piano, violin and violoncello that Mozart left us. Chopin was very fond of it and often played it at his concerts in the Salle Pleyel in Paris.

In 1788, Mozart wrote two other trios for Michael Puchberg, the first in C Major, K. 548, finished on July 14th, and the second in G Major, K. 564, completed on October 27th. Both of them are somewhat inferior pieces.

\*　\*　\*

**1. Allegro**   The first subject of this perfectly balanced movement contains chromatic thirds which endow it with an unforgettable personality. The general atmosphere is one of serenity. The piano never drowns out the violin — although it has the most interesting of the three parts. (As for the violoncello, whenever it makes itself heard, it seems happy merely to imitate the violin: it has even less to say than the viola in the 'Skittles' Trio.) This is a most exquisitely light-hearted *allegro,* noteworthy for both its spontaneity and its flights of tenderness.

**2. Andante grazioso in A Major**   This dreamy and poetical piece is remarkable for its refined harmonies and delicate contrapuntal effects. It contains a mysterious and somewhat melancholy episode in A Minor.

**3. Allegro**   Mozart originally sketched out sixty-five bars of a contrapuntal piece for this *allegro,* but in the end he abandoned this complicated beginning in favour of simpler ideas. This finale is full of freshness and vigorous gaiety — despite a short and somewhat tightly-knit passage in C Sharp Minor.

# 1788

## 38
## Symphony
## in E Flat Major,
## No. 39,
## K. 543

1. Adagio; allegro
2. Andante in A Flat Major
3. Minuet and trio
4. Allegro

During this period, when he was engulfed in poverty and apparently forgotten, Mozart accomplished one of the most extraordinary feats imaginable. Over a three month span he produced no less than twelve works — five of which, by themselves, would have sufficed to assure his immortality.

June 22nd:      Trio for piano, violin and violoncello in
                E Major, K. 542
June 26th:      Symphony in E Flat Major, No. 39,
                K. 543
June 26th:      March in D Major, K. 544 (which has
                been lost)

| | |
|---|---|
| June 26th: | Piano Sonata in C Major, K. 545 |
| June 26th: | Adagio and Fugue for strings in C Minor, K. 546 |
| July 10th: | Sonata for piano and violin in F Major, K. 547 |
| July 14th: | Trio for piano, violin and violoncello in C Major, K. 548 |
| July 16th: | *Canzonetta* 'Piu non si trovano', K. 549 |
| July 25th: | Symphony in G Minor, No. 40, K. 550 |
| August 10th: | Symphony in C Major, No. 41, K. 551 ('Jupiter') |
| August 11th: | *Lied* 'Dem hohen Kaiser-Worte treu', K. 552 |
| September 27th: | Divertimento in E Flat Major, K. 563 |

This accomplishment is extraordinary not only because several of these works are extremely complicated, but also because they are all so remarkably different from one another. They are all full of bold harmonies and they seem to have been jotted down almost without a single correction.

During this summer of 1788, Mozart must have worked at his compositions from morning until night. His works were already partially ripened in his head; they came to life and took their definitive shapes during the process of being committed to paper.

In 1815, the critic Johann Friedrich Rochlitz published several articles on Mozart in which he stated that the composer himself had assured him he had no specific method of working — which was perfectly true. For example, when Mozart sent his sister the Fantasia and Fugue in C Major, K. 394, in the accompanying letter he related how he had *written* the fugue while he was actually *composing* the fantasia (or prelude) in his head.

He would compose anywhere — on a trip, while out for a walk, or in bed at night when he could not sleep.

Of the ideas which came into his head, he kept only those which pleased him. These he would sing to himself until they took shape, developed and became clearer. Thus, he did his composing in his head. Even in the case of a long piece, Mozart was able to envisage the work immediately as a finished entity in much the same way as one takes in a large painting. His best moments were those when he succeeded in "hearing" the entire composition inside his head.

His last three symphonies represent the peak of Mozart's instrumental work. It is unlikely that they were written in preparation for the winter season of 1788-89 because at that time Mozart was no longer giving concerts and he was even having difficulty in finding pupils. In his letters to Michael Puchberg, he begged his friend to let his circle of friends know that Mozart was still teaching.

In writing his last three symphonies, Mozart was obeying an irresistible impulse as well as an exacting aesthetic need. They differ from each other far too much to have been intended as a trilogy. They have nothing in common except their admirable structure. Even their orchestrations are different: clarinets but no oboes in the Symphony in E Flat Major; oboes and clarinets but no trumpets or kettledrums in the Symphony in G Minor; and no clarinets in the 'Jupiter' Symphony.

\* \* \*

**1. Adagio; allegro**   In this movement, Mozart the skilled theatrical craftsman offers us a splendid curtain-raiser before presenting his *allegro:* the solemn, mysterious and dissonant *adagio.* The action proper begins with the *allegro,* which is a lovely, limpid piece of music — although it is also rich in lively episodes. It exudes a bewitching charm stemming from the poetry and sheer nobility of the piece. The absence of the oboes gives the woodwinds a warmer tone.

**2. Andante in A Flat Major**   At the beginning, a peaceful march theme is stated by the strings alone. Then the woodwinds take it up and their unforgettable tones begin to haunt the movement, which Mozart has written in rondo form. Between the two repetitions of the rondo-theme — both fully varied — Mozart presents us with a stormy episode twice over: first in F minor, then in the distant key of B minor. The end of the movement comes with somewhat startling suddenness.

**3. Minuet and trio**   Here we have a virile, rustic minuet. The trio, based on a simple folk tune, produces some delightful barrel-organ effects.

**4. Allegro**   The single theme of this movement in sonata form is presented in harmonic colours that change continually. Throughout the exposition it is gay and animated, but it becomes gradually more solemn during the development and loses some of its high spirits. The mounting tension is not relieved until the coda. The dramatic elements of this movement make it sound like the overture for an opera.

# 39
# Symphony in G Minor, No. 40, K. 550

1788

1. Allegro molto
2. Andante in E Flat Major
3. Minuet; trio in G Major
4. Allegro assai

The day after he finished the Symphony in E Flat Major — ten days after he borrowed 200 florins from Michael Puchberg — Mozart wrote again to his friend.

"Most honourable Brother of the Order, Dearest, most beloved Friend! I have been expecting to go to town myself one of these days and to be able to thank you in person for the kindness you have shown me. But now I should not even have the courage to appear before you, as I am obliged to tell you frankly that it is impossible for me to pay back so soon the money you have lent me and that I must beg you to be patient with me! I am very much distressed that your circumstances at the moment prevent you from assisting me as much as I could wish, for my position is so serious that I am unavoidably obliged to raise money somehow. But, good God, in whom can I confide? In no one but you, my best friend! If you would only be so kind as to get the money for me through some other channel! I shall willingly pay the interest and whoever lends it to me will, I believe, have sufficient security in my character and my income. I am only grieved to be in such an extremity; but that is the very reason why I should like a *fairly substantial* sum for a *somewhat longer period,* I mean, in order to be able to prevent a recurrence of this state of affairs. If you, my most worthy brother, do not help me in this predicament, I shall lose my honour and my *credit,* which of all things I wish to preserve. I rely entirely on your genuine friendship and brotherly love and confidently expect that you will stand by me in word and deed. If my wish is fulfilled, I can breathe freely again, because I shall then be able to put my affairs in order and *keep them so.* Do come and see me. I am always at home. During the ten days since I came to live here I have done more work than in two months in my former quarters, and if such black thoughts did not come to me so often, thoughts which I banish by a tremendous effort, things would be even better, for my rooms are pleasant — comfortable — and — *cheap.* I shall not detain you any longer with my drivel but shall *stop talking* — and *hope.* Ever your grateful servant, true friend and Brother, W. A. Mozart, 27 June 1788."

It was in these quarters, which Mozart insisted were so comfortable and where he even had a garden, that his six-month-old little daughter Theresia died on July 29th.

Despite his sorrows and despite his worries, Mozart kept

Wolfgang Amadè Mozart

working. On July 14th he wrote the Trio for piano, violin and violoncello in C Major, K. 548, for Michael Puchberg. Notwithstanding its faultless construction, this work is decidedly less personal than the Trio in E Major of the month before.

Finally, on July 25th, Mozart finished a work which has aroused more comment than almost any other, and which some authorities consider to be the first manifestation of German musical romanticism: the Symphony in G Minor, K. 550.

As in all Mozart's works of a highly chromatic character, this piece exudes great sadness. However, it would be quite wrong to dwell on the sadness in this beautiful symphony which is so rich in original melodies and harmonic surprises.

Here, the setting undergoes a radical change. The serenity and optimism of the Symphony in E Flat Major have given way to feverishness and nervousness. According to his sister-in-law Sophie Haibel, Mozart was a highly-strung man, with a most attractive disposition, although he always appeared to be plunged in the deepest of thoughts. He maintained intelligent conversation with people and his answers were always to the point. However, he seemed to be constantly absorbed in some intellectual occupation. At the table, for instance, he was often so deep in thought that he would unconsciously wring his napkin in his hands. In short, he was always in motion, always playing with things such as his hat, watch-chain, or drumming on the back of the chairs as on a keyboard.

\* \* \*

The key of G Minor, and the continual agitation of the Fortieth Symphony (there is little or no repose even in the slow movement) make it a highly original work. In it, Mozart gives free rein to the expression of his own personality, without a thought for *galant* stylistic formalities. However, he never commits excesses of any sort, nor oversteps the bounds of classical rigour. Three of the four movements are in sonata form, and the developments have been kept very short.

Excess, in every one of its forms, was distasteful to Mozart, thus he never stooped to exaggeration or vulgarity. The means by which he achieved perfection are accuracy of expression, neatness of form and structural balance.

\* \* \*

**1. Allegro molto**   (Mozart originally marked the beginning of this movement *allegro assai*). The first rhythmic and tense theme is stated abruptly, with no preamble. After a brief pause, the strings and then the woodwinds present the second subject (in B Flat Major). There is scarcely a moment's repose in the movement. The closely-knit development is drawn entirely from the first subject. After an admirable passage leading up to the recapitulation, Mozart displays his thematic material once again, in a different guise. Eight bars of a poignant sweetness lull the listener for a moment into the belief that he is about to enjoy a period of calm — but the movement ends as it began, in feverish agitation.

**2. Andante in E Flat Major**   Nor does this movement bring any relaxation. Its rhythm seems to pant breathlessly (Mozart makes use of insistent demi-semi-quavers), and the general mood is intense. The music is melancholy, with constant modulations into minor keys. There are discords, superimposed rhythms, displaced accents. As in the opening *allegro*, the development is prolonged into the recapitulation and the listener encounters a number of very beautiful surprises.

**3. Minuet; trio in G Major**   Here we have an impatient, aggressive minuet. The trio presents a striking contrast — it is a graceful pastorale.

**4. Allegro assai**   In this energetic, quivering movement, inexorable answers are given to a series of urgent questions. After an affirmative and rhythmically harsh restatement of the first subject, we move to the development, which leads to a vigorous and tightly-knit *fugato*. Despite the reduced orchestration — there are no trumpets or kettledrums — the Symphony in G Minor gives a continuing impression of strength.

# 40

**1788**

# Symphony in C Major, No. 41, K. 551 ('Jupiter')

1. Allegro vivace
2. Andante cantabile in F Major
3. Minuet and trio
4. Allegro molto

Early in July, Mozart wrote to Michael Puchberg once again. His financial problems were becoming more pressing all the time and he was in desperate straits.

"Dearest friend and B.O. Owing to great difficulties and complications my affairs have become so involved that it is of the utmost importance to raise some money on these two pawnbroker's tickets. In the name of our friendship I implore you to do me this favour; but you must do it immediately. Forgive my importunity, but you know my situation. Ah! If only you had done what I asked you! Do it even now — then everything will be as I desire. Ever your, Mozart."

Why did Puchberg refuse to lend the largish sum that Mozart was asking? It is tempting to accuse the rich Viennese merchant of stinginess. However, though he lent Mozart only a little, he *did* lend him money.

In his last letter to Nannerl, on August 2nd, Mozart apologized for not having sent her his congratulations on her name-day.

" . . . you know very well that I am rather lazy about letter-writing. So do not take it amiss, if I *seldom* write to you. But this must not prevent you from writing very often to *me*. Indeed, though I detest writing letters, I love getting them. Moreover, you have far more to write about than I have, for Salzburg affairs interest me more than what is happening in Vienna can interest you."

On August 10th, Mozart finished the Symphony in C Major — his last work in symphonic form.

\* \* \*

The instrumentation for the Symphony in C Major includes a flute, two oboes, two bassoons, two horns, two trumpets, kettledrums and strings. In this work, which sounds so bright, clear and resonant compared with the dark-hued Symphony in G Minor, Mozart deliberately dispenses with the clarinets. Nor does he add them later, as he had previously when he finished composing the Fortieth Symphony. For the 'Jupiter' Symphony, he had this particular instrumental colouring in mind all along.

Incidentally, it is not known how this work came to be called the 'Jupiter' Symphony.

# 1788 ('Jupiter')

* * *

**1. Allegro vivace**   The Symphony in E Flat Major opened with a prelude full of mystery. The Symphony in G Minor plunged the listener into drama from the outset. The Symphony in C Major begins, as do so many other symphonies of Mozart's, with an imperious call which establishes the vital exuberance of the piece. The sentiments expressed in this movement are joyful, grandiose, even heroic; they are never emotional. The superhuman energy which Mozart displays here is adequate justification in itself for the Olympian appellation which has been given to this symphony.

**2. Andante cantabile in F Major**   This is a noble song, punctuated by incessant oppositions of *piano* and *forte* markings. The music has a depth of humanity which must inevitably bring to mind what Constanze once said of Mozart. "It was impossible not to love him, he was so good!" The violins and violas are muted, the trumpets and kettledrums remain silent. An episode in D Minor provides a moment or two of disquiet, but the movement closes in a mood of majestic calm.

**3. Minuet and trio**   This solemn minuet is weighed-down by its chromatic effects. In the trio, Mozart already sounds the four notes of the initial theme of the finale.

**4. Allegro molto**   This theme of four notes is a motif of liturgical origin frequently used by early 18th century polyphonists. Mozart must have been fascinated by this model of simplicity. The movement contains three other important themes. After the fugal elaboration of the development, the four themes are played simultaneously by the full orchestra (Bars 387 to 390). With its unusual strength and impetuosity, this finale is without parallel in the history of music. Mozart wrote it in one session with scarcely a correction anywhere. Its radiant beauty is a fitting end to Mozart's career as a composer of symphonies. In the pages of this absolutely perfect finale, he managed to give polyphonic composition a lightness and vivacity unknown at the time of Bach and Handel.

# 1788

## 41

## Divertimento for string trio in E Flat Major, K. 563

1. Allegro
2. Adagio in A Flat Major
3. Minuet and trio
4. Andante in B Flat Major
5. Minuet: trio I in A Flat Major;
   trio II in B Flat Major
6. Allegro

Why did Mozart write three new symphonies when he had virtually no hope of hearing them played? Who was there who could even be shown these works, which he knew himself to be both original and important? Constanze? Michael Puchberg?

At the end of the summer of 1788, Mozart's artistic solitude and his social isolation seemed complete. Vienna ignored him. At thirty-two years of age, he had failed to secure the patronage he desperately needed from the influential people of the world who could assure his peace of mind and his material security. To cap his misery, neither Constanze's health nor his own was particularly good.

On August 11th, the day after he finished writing the Symphony in C Major, he wrote a *lied*, 'Dem hohen Kaiser-Worte treu', K. 552, which was inspired by the war against the Turks. Following that, he stopped composing completely for a period of six weeks.

He emerged from his silence on September 27th to write a work for Michael Puchberg which stands alone in his entire output: the Divertimento for string trio in E Flat Major, K. 563.

The Divertimento clearly represents a return to the *galant* style which Mozart had abandoned more than ten years earlier. Actually, the only *galant* thing about this work is its format. Its unusual instrumental combination, its refined scoring and most of all its depth of expression combine to raise it above the level of a simple divertimento and indicate very clearly that here is a piece for highly skilled musicians. Although the Divertimento in E Flat Major was written during one of the unhappiest periods of Mozart's life, it shows no sign whatever of the despair he must have been feeling.

\* \* \*

**1. Allegro**  The mood of this first movement wavers unceasingly between joy and gravity. The development is short, as is appropriate in a divertimento, and offers some delightful modulations. The sonority of the string trio is more transparent and more intimate than that of the string quartet. Throughout the entire work, there is perfect agreement among the three instruments. The part of the violoncello is equally important as those of the violin and the viola — an arrangement that would have pleased the King of Prussia.

**2. Adagio in A Flat Major**  As a matter of fact, the principal theme of this movement is presented by the cello. The general mood is one of confidence and tenderness. Mozart has much to say in this graceful movement and he says it very eloquently.

**3. Minuet and trio**  A joyful, frisky minuet, in the spirit of the minuets in the Haydn Quartets. The trio is perhaps a little less demonstrative.

**4. Andante in E Flat Major**  This movement takes the form of double variations. The theme is a light, popular march in two segments. At each repetition, both segments are varied. Mozart loved writing variations and in this case he gives free rein to his imagination. Imperceptibly, he moves further and further away from the initial presentation of the march-theme. When he states it once again, in its original version in the coda, only then does the listener realize the changes it had undergone. In the third variation (which is in a minor key) the mood becomes more intimate. The fourth gives the viola an opportunity to present a solemn version of the theme, somewhat in the style of the *andante cantabile* in Haydn's 'Emperor' Quartet.

**5. Minuet; trios I and II**  This minuet is more subtle than the previous one. The first trio, in A Flat Major, is an exquisite, graceful little waltz. The second, in B Flat Major, is no less stirring. The entire movement sparkles with the spirit of truly Viennese music.

**6. Allegro** The hunting calls of this joyous rondo give it a vital impulse. This music provides the senses with a delightful pleasure.

**Works written between September 27th, 1788 and September 29th, 1789**

*Trio for piano, violin and violoncello in G Major, K. 564*
*Instrumentation of Handel's 'Acis and Galatea', K. 566*
*Six German Dances for orchestra, K. 567*
*Twelve Minuets for orchestra, K. 568*
*Piano Sonata in B Flat Major, K. 570*
*Six German Dances for orchestra, K. 571*

*Instrumentation of Handel's 'Messiah', K. 572*
*Piano Variations in D Major, K. 573*
*Gigue for piano in G Major, K. 574*
*String Quartet in D Major, K. 575 (Prussian No. 1)*
*Piano Sonata in D Major, K. 576*
*Arias for Soprano:*
    *'Al desio di chi t'adora', K. 577*
    *'Alma grande e nobil core', K. 578*
    *'Un moto di gioia', K. 579*
    *'Schon lacht der Holde Frühling', K. 580*

# 1789

## 42
## Quintet for clarinet and strings in A Major, K. 581

1. Allegro
2. Larghetto in D Major
3. Minuet; trio I in A Minor; trio II in A Major
4. Allegretto con variazioni

After his creative outburst during the summer of 1788, the rhythm of Mozart's productivity slowed considerably for a period of nearly a year. Indeed, after finishing a third trio for Michael Puchberg in October, he fell silent — this time for a long period. However, the lack of commissions and the virtual impossibility of arranging to have his work performed did not prevent his acquitting himself honourably as Court composer. He wrote several German dances and minuets at the end of the year for the masked balls held in the Redoutensaal. During January, 1789, however, no new work is listed in his thematic catalogue.

In February, Mozart composed the Piano Sonata in B Flat Major, K. 570. This is a work of no great importance. It was published with a violin accompaniment which was not even his. During the same month, he wrote the six German Dances, K. 571. The trio in the second of these is an exquisite little waltz in A Minor, in true Viennese style. He also devoted himself to other work — for example, the reinstrumentation of several Handel oratorios, for Baron van Swieten.

In November 1788, Mozart reorchestrated 'Acis and Galatea'; a public performance of it was given for his benefit. In March, 1789, he did the same thing for 'Messiah'. Later, in 1790, he reorchestrated 'Alexander's Feast' and 'Ode for St. Cecilia's Day'. His work included the shortening of some of the arias and the transcription of the original organ parts for wind instruments.

Mozard openly admired Handel. He always said no one knew better than Handel how to contrive his effects, even though he was often "rather fastidious, as was the fashion in those days".

Despite certain fees paid by Baron van Swieten, Mozart's financial situation had not improved. He was embarrassed at having to turn to Puchberg continually and he asked a certain Franz Hofdemel for help. Hofdemel, who was the husband of one of Mozart's pupils, lent him a little money. The receipt Mozart sent him is dated April 2nd.

It then developed that Prince Karl Lichnowsky, another of Mozart's pupil. (and a future patron of Beethoven) had to go to Berlin on business. He invited Mozart to join him.

262

Mozart accepted, feeling that in his present state he had nothing to lose.

His past experiences seemed to have taught him nothing. Off he set once again to try and make his fortune elsewhere, this time with Hofdemel's money in his pocket and dread in his heart.

As an economy measure, Michael Puchberg took Constanze and Karl into his house and during the trip Mozart used Puchberg's address for all his letters to his wife. Constanze was at this point pregnant for the fifth time; the baby was expected in November.

Mozart set out on April 8th, 1789. He had not been away from Vienna since he returned from Prague in November 1787, following the production of 'Don Giovanni'. He sent his first message to Constanze that very evening. Over the next two months he sent her many tender, affectionate letters. Constanze always took a long time to reply and he complained bitterly about this to her.

"Dearest little wife, if only I had a letter from you! If I were to tell you all the things I do with your dear portrait, I think that you would often laugh. For instance, when I take it out of its case, I say, 'Good-day Stanzerl! — Good-day little rascal, pussy-pussy, little turned-up nose, little bagatelle, Schluck und Druck', and when I put it away again, I let it slip in very slowly, saying all the time, ' Nu — Nu — Nu — Nu!' with the peculiar *emphasis* which this word so full of meaning demands, and then just at the last, quickly, 'Good night, little mouse, sleep well'. "

Later, in 'The Magic Flute', Mozart has Tamino sing, as he gazes at Pamina's portrait, "Dies Bildnis ist bezaubernd

*Mozart, aged 33.  Dresden,*
*April 17th, 1789.  Silverpoint sketch*
*by Dora Stock.*

schön . . . " ('This portrait of enchanting beauty . . . ')

On April 10th, Prince Lichnowsky and Mozart were in Prague, and on the 12th in Dresden, where Mozart called on the singer Josepha Duschek. As a joke, he did not give his name when the door was opened, but his old friend Mme. Duschek recognized him through the window and she came to greet him with the words, "Why here comes someone who is very like Mozart".

He played his Divertimento, K. 563, at a concert and accompanied Mme. Duschek in several arias from his operas. It was a triumphal evening. It had been a long time since Mozart had given a concert and he was delighted to feel himself appreciated again.

It was during Mozart's visit to Dresden that Dora Stock made her silver-crayon drawing of Mozart. The sketch shows him in profile with a broad forehead, prominent nose, somewhat bitter mouth and receding chin.

After Dresden, the travellers' next stop was Leipzig.

As soon as they reached the town, Mozart called at the Thomasschule, which had become famous through its association with Johann Sebastian Bach. He was received by the Director, Johann Friedrich Doles, then 74 years old, who had been one of Bach's pupils.

On April 22nd, Mozart aroused general admiration when he gave a concert at the Thomaskirche on Bach's own organ. To thank him, Doles let him hear a motet by Johann Sebastian which was hitherto unknown to Mozart, ' Singet dem Herrn ein neues Lied'.

Mozart was very impressed and he cried out, "Here, for

once, is something from which one may learn!"

On the 25th the travellers arrived at Potsdam where Mozart hoped to be noticed by Friedrich Wilhelm II, the King of Prussia. The King had the same love for the violoncello that his uncle, Frederick the Great, had for the flute. He knew and admired Mozart's string quartets and he immediately commissioned the composer to write six of them in addition to several "easy" piano sonatas for his eldest daughter, Princess Friederike. But he did not offer Mozart a post at his Court.

Mozart spent a week at Potsdam where he made friends, several of whom organized musical evenings in his honour.

In May, rather than return to Vienna with Lichnowsky, Mozart went on alone to Leipzig, where he gave a concert on the 12th. At the rehearsal, he beat time so energetically that the buckle broke on one of his shoes. The programme consisted of one of his symphonies (for which the orchestra already had the music), two concertos and the dramatic *scena* 'Chi'io mi scordi di te?', sung by Josepha Duschek, with the composer at the piano.

On May 19th, Mozart was in Berlin. On the evening of his arrival, there was a performance of 'The Abduction from the Seraglio'. The story goes that Mozart slipped into the theatre incognito but he was recognized by the audience and was given a standing ovation.

Another story has it that during his stay in Berlin he had an affair with the singer Henriette Baranius.

One thing that is certain, however, is that on May 23rd Mozart wrote to Constanze, "First of all, my darling little

1789
        *Quintet for clarinet and strings in*
        *A Major, K. 581*

wife, when I return you must be more delighted with having me back than with the money I shall bring. A hundred friedrichs d'or are not nine hundred gulden but seven hundred — at least that is what they have told me here. Secondly, Lichnowsky (as he was in a hurry) left me here, and so I have had to pay for my keep in Potsdam, which is an expensive place. Thirdly, I had to lend him a hundred gulden, as his purse was getting empty. I could not well refuse him: you will know why."

Mozart could not possibly foresee his future glory. Certainly, he never dreamed that one day his correspondence would be published and the secrets he confided to his wife would be betrayed.

Mozart's letters to Constanze during this trip, like those from Frankfurt later in 1790, and the ones he sent to her in Baden in 1791, show how deeply he loved her. He harped continually at his sadness at being separated from her and his desire to find himself back in her arms before long. He sent her a thousand bits of advice about her health, a thousand hugs and a thousand kisses — often with naughty little words which betray the secrets of their intimate conversations. In this same letter of May 23rd, he wrote: "Arrange your dear sweet nest very daintily, for my little fellow deserves it indeed, he has really behaved himself very well and is only longing to possess your sweetest . . ."

On June 4th, Mozart returned to Vienna. From an artistic point of view, the trip brought him only success. He had been applauded everywhere his music had been played — especially in Leipzig, where Bach had died in 1750. But he came back with his pockets empty. So he settled down to the task of writing, as quickly as possible, the first of the six string quartets which Friedrich Wilhelm II had commissioned (only three of which were finished when he died) along with the first of the "easy" piano sonatas (it is anything but easy) for the Princess. He was paid promptly for his work.

The money arrived in the nick of time. Constanze was suffering from an infected foot, and then Mozart himself fell seriously ill. His wife's pregnancy increased his anxiety. He had to have the doctor come and see them and he had to pay the pharmacy. In short, the king's money was quickly spent.

Mozart wrote to Michael Puchberg, in desperation:

"Dearest, most beloved Friend and most honourable B.O. Great God! I would not wish my worst enemy to be in my present position. And if you, most beloved friend and brother, forsake me, we are altogether lost, *both my unfortunate and blameless self* and my poor sick wife and child . . . I need not tell you once more that owing to my unfortunate illness I have been prevented from earning anything. But I must mention that in spite of my wretched condition I decided to give subscription concerts at home in order to be able to meet at least my present great and frequent expenses, for I was absolutely convinced of your friendly assistance. But even this has failed. Unfortunately, Fate is so much against me, *though only in Vienna,* that even when I want to, I cannot make any money. A fortnight ago I sent round a list for subscribers and so far the only name on it is that of the Baron van Swieten! . . .

Dearest, most beloved friend and brother — you know *my present circumstances,* but you also know *my prospects.* So let things remain as we arranged; that is, thus or thus, you understand what I mean. Meanwhile I am composing six easy clavier sonatas for Princess Friederike and six quartets for the King, all of which Kozeluch is engraving at my expense ... In a month or two my fate must be decided *in every detail.* Therefore, most beloved friend, you will not be risking anything so far as I am concerned. So it all depends, my only friend, upon whether you will or can lend me another 500 gulden. Until my affairs are settled, I undertake to pay back ten gulden a month; and then, as this is bound to happen in a few months, I shall pay back the whole sum with whatever interest you may demand, at the same time acknowledge myself to be your debtor for life. That, alas, I shall have to remain, for I shall never be able to thank you sufficiently for your friendship and affection. Thank God, that is over. Now you know all. Do not be offended by my confiding in you and remember that unless you help me, the honour, the peace of mind and perhaps the very life of your friend and brother Mason will be ruined.

Ever your most grateful servant, true friend and brother W. A. Mozart."

On the day that Mozart wrote this letter, July 14th, 1789, the Sansculottes stormed the Bastille in Paris.

Puchberg made no reply and on the 17th Mozart wrote to him again, sick with worry.

"I fear you are angry with me, for you are not sending me a reply! ... I beg and implore you, in God's name, for whatever temporary assistance you can give me and also for your advice and comforting sympathy.

Ever your most grateful servant          Mozart

PS. — My wife was wretchedly ill again yesterday. Today leeches were applied and she is, thank God, somewhat better. I am indeed most unhappy, and am forever hovering between hope and fear!"

Puchberg was sufficiently moved to send Mozart 150 florins. But Dr. Closset, who was looking after Constanze, recommended that she take the waters at Baden. Puchberg's money was not going to go very far.

Suddenly, during August, a revival of 'The Marriage of Figaro' was announced — no doubt because the echoes of the French Revolution had reached Vienna and aroused renewed interest in this work. Mozart hardly dared believe his good fortune.

Adriana Ferrarese del Bene (who was Lorenzo da Ponte's mistress) was to sing Susanna. Mozart wrote two new arias for her: 'Al desio di chi t'adora', which was intended to replace 'Deh vieni, non tardar', and an *arietta* in G Major, 'Un moto di gioia'. We do not know exactly where this *arietta* came in the score.

The revival of 'Figaro' opened on August 29th and was an immense success. By the end of 1789, the opera had been sung at least a dozen times. Joseph II took the opportunity to commission an *opera buffa* from Mozart for the 1790 Carnival.

A month later, on September 29th, just as he was beginning work on his libretto of 'Cosi fan tutte' with Lorenzo da

Ponte, Mozart wrote the Quintet for clarinet and strings in A major, K. 581, for his friend and fellow Mason, the clarinettist Anton Stadler.

\* \* \*

**1. Allegro** This movement has three main themes: the first is rather solemn; the second is tenderly melancholic; the third moves along in a purposeful manner. The clarinet gives a sparkling performance without ever making a display of its own virtuosity. To allow it to play the lead role without undue ostentation, Mozart uses the strings with infinite restraint and gentleness. The listener cannot help but admire the simple, sparse structure of this *allegro*.

**2. Larghetto in D Major** This nocturne gives the clarinet an incomparably beautiful song to sing, intersected with the passionate tones of the first violin. It is a song of tenderness and of brotherhood.

**3. Minuet; trios I and II** The minuet is a model of conciseness. The first trio, in A Minor, is played by the strings alone. The second, in A Major, adopts the style of a country dance — all peaceful joy and sweet emotion.

**4. Allegretto with variations** Before writing this finale, Mozart sketched out 89 bars of quite a different movement. He abandoned this rough draft (which he used later on for 'Cosi') and wrote five variations and a stirring coda on a brisk little march theme. The first variation allows the clarinet to exhibit its agility while the strings repeat the initial theme. In the second variation, the clarinet demonstrates the full range of its register. The third variation, in

A Minor, is given over to the viola which sings a plaintive melody. Gaiety returns with the fourth variation, in A Major. In the fifth variation, marked *adagio*, the clarinet sings two poignant chromatic phrases which are among the most beautiful melodic ideas ever expressed by Mozart. After a short transition, interspersed with silences (mindful of a Masonic ritual), the work is brought to a close by a lively, sprightly and witty coda.

**Works written between September 29th, 1789 and January 26th, 1790**

*Aria for soprano 'Chi sa, chi sa, qual sia', K. 582*
*Aria for soprano 'Vado, ma dove?', K. 583*
*Aria for bass 'Rivolgete a lui', K. 584*
*Twelve Minuets for orchestra, K. 585*
*Twelve German Dances, K. 586*
*Contredanse for orchestra, K. 587 ('Koburg')*

# 1790 | 43 'Cosi fan tutte', K. 588

For the third and last time, Mozart made use of the services and talents of the brilliant Lorenzo da Ponte. It was not long before da Ponte handed over the excellent libretto of 'Cosi fan tutte'. For his part, Mozart worked at the score over a period of four months, while still attending to other business.

In October, 1789, he wrote two arias for Louise Villeneuve, who was to sing Dorabella in 'Cosi fan tutte'. These were to be included in an opera by da Ponte and Martin y Soler, 'Il Burbero di buon core'. The second aria, 'Vado, ma dove?', is exquisite in its refinement and its lean, sparse structure reminds the listener strongly of the Quintet for clarinet and strings in A Major.

On November 16th, Constanze gave birth to a girl, Anna, who only lived for one hour. It was a difficult birth which left Constanze very weak.

While he was still busy working on 'Cosi fan tutte', Mozart wrote several German dances and minuets in preparation for the year-end festivities and the 1790 Carnival.

In mid-December, as was his custom, Prince Nicholas Esterhazy arrived in Vienna to spend a few weeks in his house on Wallnerstrasse. Naturally, Joseph Haydn formed part of his entourage.

A day or two later, on December 18th, one of Haydn's operas, 'La Fedelta premiata', was performed at the Kärntnertor-Theater. It was sung in a German version by Schikaneder and it is not unreasonable to imagine that Mozart made a point of attending to applaud his friend's work.

Mozart was financially embarrassed by the expenses incurred in connection with Constanze's delivery and convalescence and on the 29th he wrote yet again to Michael Puchberg asking to borrow money.

"Do not be alarmed at the contents of this letter. Only to you, most beloved friend, who know everything about me and my circumstances, have I the courage to open my heart completely. According to the present arrangement, I am to receive from the management next month 200 ducats for my opera. If you can and will lend me 400 gulden until then, you will be rescuing your friend from the greatest embarrassment; and I give you my word of honour that by that time you will have the money back in full and with many thanks ... I know only too well how much I owe you! I beg you to be patient a little longer in regard to my old debts. I shall certainly repay you, that I promise on my honour. Once more I beg you, rescue me just this time from my horrible situation. As soon as I get the money for my opera, you shall have the 400 gulden back for certain. And this summer, thanks to my work for the King of Prussia, I hope to be able to convince you completely of my honesty. Contrary to our arrangement we cannot have any music at our house tomorrow — I have too much work ... But I invite you, you alone, to come along on Thursday at 10 o'clock in the morning to hear a short rehearsal of my opera. I am only inviting Haydn and yourself. I shall tell you when we meet about Salieri's plots, which, however, have completely failed already. Adieu. Ever your grateful friend and brother,

W. A. Mozart"

The first rehearsal of 'Cosi fan tutte' with the orchestra took place on January 21st, 1790, with both Haydn and Puchberg present. The new opera opened on the 26th, under Mozart's direction.

The parts of the two sisters in the play, Dorabella and Fiordiligi, were sung respectively by Louise Villeneuve and Adriana Ferrarese del Bene (who were also sisters in real life). The original Figaro, Francesco Benucci, played the part of Guglielmo, while the parts of Ferrando and Don Alfonso were taken by Vincenzo Calvesi and Francesco Bussani. Bussani's wife, Sardi, (who created the part of Cherubino in 'Figaro') sang the role of Despina.

Next morning the 'Luxus und Mode Journal' carried a report to the effect that an excellent new work by Mozart had been presented on the stage of the National Imperial Theatre. "As to the music", the writer ended, "what more need one say than that it was by Mozart?"

The translation of 'Cosi fan tutte, ossia la Scuola degli Amanti', in the Oxford Companion to Music reads, 'That's what they all do' or 'The School for Lovers'.

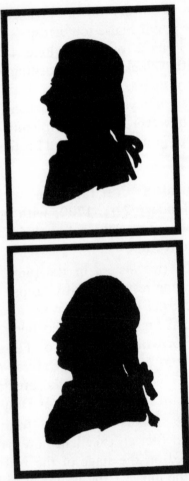

*Francesco Benucci and Vincenzo Calvesi, creators of the
roles of Guglielmo and Ferrando in 'Cosi fan tutte'.
Silhouettes by Löschenkohl.*

# 1790

'Cosi' is a perfect comedy of deceit and trickery, set in Naples in 1790. It deals with three couples: a pair of accomplices (Don Alfonso and Despina); a pair of sentimental lovers (Fiordiligi and Guglielmo); and another pair of lovers, who are more prosaic, (Dorabella and Ferrando).

The plot holds to the classical rule of unity of time, place and action; it is very simple. Don Alfonso is an old roué who declares that all women are unfaithful. His friends Guglielmo and Ferrando, who are officers, make a bet with him, confident in the absolute virtue of their respective fiancées, Fiordiligi and Dorabella. They pretend to go off to the war, but they return immediately disguised as Albanians, and, with the complicity of Don Alfonso and Despina the soubrette, each manages to seduce the other's fiancée. No sooner have the marriage contracts been signed than the whole kettle of fish is uncovered. Naturally, the two pairs of lovers fall out with each other but they are reconciled before the final curtain.

It was rumoured that it was Joseph II himself who suggested the subject of 'Cosi fan tutte' to Mozart — and indeed, even insisted on it. On the other hand, since this is by no means the first instance of an *opera buffa* having to do with the misfortunes of two pairs of lovers who fall victim to the machinations of a diabolical character, we may equally well suppose that da Ponte was inspired by similar plots written earlier than 'Cosi'.

The 19th Century was a period during which womanly virtue was taken rather seriously. To hold it up to ridicule involved certain hazards. Critics were therefore vigorous in their denunciations of the "unpardonable stupidity" of this opera. Beethoven and Wagner were scandalized by it, and Barbier and Carré, the librettists of 'Faust', went to great lengths in their attempts to adapt Mozart's music to Shakespeare's comedy, 'Love's Labour Lost'.

In 'Cosi fan tutte', an opera which is pre-eminently misogynist in character, love and women are pilloried with pitiless cynicism. The people of the 19th Century found little amusement in the comedy precisely because it is the falseness and the insincerity which give it its own special charm. Indeed, the principal fault of the libretto is that it is impossible to take the characters seriously.

It is in vain that Mozart expresses an incredibly rich gamut of emotions in a dazzling parody of human relationships. The fact is that the 'people' who are experiencing the emotions at issue are really puppets and one is hard put to it to take their feelings seriously.

In 'Cosi fan tutte', everything is exaggerated and larger than life. But the parody is so crafty and the imitation of real life is so perfect that one is occasionally surprised to find oneself doubting it.

Mozart, forced as he was to accept this artificial libretto, decided, consequently, to stake everything on the music.

From the viewpoints of vocal accompaniment and orchestration, 'Cosi fan tutte' may well be Mozart's most beautiful score; it is certainly the most sensual. His use of woodwinds is exceptionally successful — particularly the voluptuous clarinets.

The orchestra assumes the role of commentator. It takes

a very intimate part in the action, following the characters step by step, lieing, laughing and weeping with them; it judges them harshly and mocks them pitilessly. More than any other of Mozart's operas, 'Cosi fan tutte' is an opera of ensembles. There are six duets, five trios, one quartet, two quintets, one sextet, one chorus and two grand finales with chorus. There are only thirteen solos. With its thirty-one numbers, it is the longest of Mozart's lyric works. Its compression into two acts and its lack of action make it seem even longer. Each of the six characters has two solo songs, except for Ferrando, who has three. The most meagre character from a musical point of view is Don Alfonso, although he is the most important character in the plot. His two arias, 'Vorrei dir, e cor non ho' (No. 5), and 'Tutti accusan le donne' (No. 30), are perfectly in tune with the spirit of the character — cynical and brittle.

Despina's two songs, 'In uomini, in soldati' (No. 2) and 'Una donna a quindici anni' (No. 19), are light, gay and provocative. They serve as models for soubrette's songs in future Viennese operettas.

The role of Fiordiligi is the one Mozart flattered most, doubtless because the actress playing it was Lorenzo da Ponte's mistress. She sings 'Come scoglio immoto' (No. 14), a difficult aria full of hazardous leaps designed to show off the range of her voice; and also the brilliant rondo 'Per pieta, ben mio, perdona' (No. 25), with its obbligato for two horns.

Dorabella has two arias. The first, 'Smanie implacabili'

(No. 11), which parodies the tragic aria from an *opera seria*, is admirable for its deceitful passion and false nobility. The second, 'E amore un ladroncello' (No. 28), leaves the listener strangely unmoved.

Guglielmo's first aria, 'Non siate ritrosi' (No. 15), is superior to the longer, less polished 'Rivolgete a lui lo sguardo', K. 584, which Mozart wrote previously, but which he finally cut out simply to avoid holding up the action of the play. Guglielmo also sings the comic aria, 'Donne mie, la fate a tanti' (No. 26), to a delightful mocking accompaniment from the orchestra. In it, he lets his friend know the disloyal Dorabella has given him her portrait in return for a little golden heart.

Ferrando's first two arias, 'Un' aura amorosa' (No. 17) and the cavatina 'Tradito schernito' (No. 27), are in the somewhat cold style of Don Ottavio's arias in 'Don Giovanni'. The third, 'Ah, lo veggio quell'anima bella' (No. 24), makes use of a theme which Mozart noted in his first draft for the finale of the Quintet for clarinet and strings, K. 581.

More than anything else, however, the exceptional beauty of 'Cosi fan tutte' lies in the ensembles. Among these, several are in the first act.

The first duet of Fiordiligi and Dorabella, 'Ah guarda, sorella' (No. 4) in which the clarinets and languorous bassoons establish the elegant, perfumed, sensual atmosphere of the two sisters' garden in which much of the action takes place; the two quintets 'Sento, o Dio' (No. 6), and especially the farewell quintet, 'Di scrivermi ogni giorno' (No. 9), which is so lovely that the listener wishes

280

desperately to believe in the sincerity of the two heroines; the exquisite little trio 'Soave sia il vento' (No. 10); and finally, the laughing trio 'E voi ridete' (No. 16) with its irresistible humour.

In the second act, the listener will admire the charming, easy grace of the duet 'Prendero quel brunettino' (No. 20); the lovely serenade 'Secondate, aurette amiche' (No. 21), sung by Ferrando and Guglielmo in a boat filled with singers and musicians; and finally, the incomparable duet between Fiordiligi and Ferrando 'Fra gli amplessi', (No. 29), which is the very image of a genuine declaration of love.

In the sextet 'Alla bella Despinetta' (No. 13), Mozart explains a complicated situation quickly and clearly. The finales of the first and second acts contain five and eight numbers respectively. A great many things occur in these finales which remain models of organization and ingenuity.

In the finale of the second act, the listener will admire a vocal quartet *(larghetto)* during which Fiordiligi, Dorabella and Ferrando drink a toast to their happiness, while Guglielmo, who is in a very bad mood, expresses the cordial wish that they will poison themselves.

This piece is in the style of certain of Mozart's comic serenades for three singers, all fashioned on the same model: serenaders, extolling love and women to the skies, interrupted in their sentimental outpourings either by a rival or by a drunkard, who sermonizes on the folly of love and the infidelity of women.

The interrupted serenade 'Liebes Mädchen', K. 441c,

written in 1783, illustrates this form of humour, by which Mozart seemed particularly amused.

**Sole work written between January 26th and June, 1790**

*String Quartet in B Flat Major, K. 589 (Prussian No. 2)*

# 44
## String Quartet
## in F Major,
## K. 590
## (Prussian No. 3)

1. **Allegro moderato**
2. **Andante in C Major**
3. **Minuet and trio**
4. **Allegro**

Mozart celebrated his thirty-fourth birthday the day after the première of 'Cosi fan tutte'.

The opera was sung four times in February. It was highly successful, although Mozart was very disappointed that illness prevented the Emperor from hearing the work he had commissioned. Indeed, the Emperor Joseph II was fated never to hear it, for he died, very suddenly, on February 20th. There was national mourning and, as of that date, all theatres were closed until April. The career of 'Cosi fan tutte' was momentarily halted.

Mozart was at the end of his resources. Once again he badgered Michael Puchberg with a long series of begging letters. At the beginning of April he wrote:

"I now stand on the threshold of my fortune; but the opportunity will be lost forever, if this time I cannot make use of it. My present circumstances however, are such that in spite of my excellent prospects I must abandon all hope of furthering my fortunes unless I can count on the help of a staunch friend. For some time you must have noticed my constant sadness — and only the very many kindnesses which you have already rendered me, have prevented me from speaking out. Now, however — once more, but for the last time — I call upon you to stand by me to the utmost of your power in this most urgent matter which is going to determine my whole happiness."

On April 8th, another letter:

"You are right, dearest friend, not to honour me with a reply! My importunity is too great. I only beg you to consider my position from every point of view, to remember my cordial friendship and my confidence in you and to forgive me! But if you can and will extricate me from a temporary embarrassment, then, for the love of God, do so!"

He returned to the charge at the beginning of May. ". . . I must have something to live on until I have arranged my concerts and until the quartets on which I am working have been sent to be engraved. So if only I had in hand 600 gulden at least, I should be able to compose with a fairly easy mind. And ah! I must have peace of mind."

Joseph II was succeeded by his brother, the Grand Duke of Tuscany, who was crowned under the name of Leopold II.

284

As soon as he ascended the throne, the new Emperor made certain changes in the personnel of his Court. Mozart retained his post as chamber musician and composer to the Court at the same pitifully small salary Joseph II had been paying him. However, Lorenzo da Ponte and his mistress Ferrarese del Bene fell into disfavour and had to leave Vienna. Mozart was most unhappy to lose his best librettist. Da Ponte went to the United States and continued his career there until his death in 1838, at the age of 89.

Salieri, the *Kapellmeister*, doubtless felt the weight of Leopold's disapproval as well. He hastened to resign his post but he managed to have his pupil Joseph Weigl appointed instead of Mozart.

Always on the look-out for a better post, and anxious to improve his financial situation, Mozart addressed a petition to the Emperor in the hope of being appointed Second *Kapellmeister*. To strengthen his request, he also wrote to Leopold's son, the Archduke Franz, at the beginning of May.

"I make so bold as to beg your Royal Highness very respectfully to use your most gracious influence with His Majesty the King with regard to my most humble petition to His Majesty. Prompted by a desire for fame, by a love of work and by a conviction of my wide knowledge, I venture to apply for the post of second Kapellmeister, particularly as Salieri, that very gifted Kapellmeister, has never devoted himself to church music, whereas from my youth up I have made myself completely familiar with this style. The slight reputation which I have acquired in the world by my pianoforte playing has encouraged me to ask His Majesty for the favour of being entrusted with the musical education of the Royal Family."

On May 17th, Mozart informed Michael Puchberg that he would have to go to a money lender.

"If you only knew what grief and worry all this causes me. It has prevented me all this time from finishing my quartets. I now have great hopes of an appointment at court, for I have reliable information that the Emperor has not sent back my petition with a favourable or damning remark, as he has the others, but has retained it. That is a good sign."

None of Mozart's approaches produced any positive result and he continued to sink deeper and deeper into his miserable state. His health was poor and he suffered from headaches. Despite his cramped quarters, he had two pupils and he persisted in asking people to let it be known that he gave lessons. Constanze was no better and early in May, on her doctor's advice, she left for Baden to take the waters.

Alone in Vienna, Mozart wrote to tell his wife that on June 1st he had gone to hear the last act of Martin y Soler's 'Una Cosa rara'. However, he preferred 'Die beiden Antons', he said, a *singspiel* by Benedikt Schack. This Schack was a flautist and singer in Schikaneder's theater company. The following year he sang the role of Tamino in 'The Magic Flute'.

Since 'Cosi fan tutte', all Mozart composed was a second string quartet for the King of Prussia — the Quartet in

B Flat Major, K. 589. In June, he finished a third, and his last string quartet, the Quartet in F Major, K. 590.

In a further letter to Puchberg, he complained:

"I have now been obliged to give away my quartets (those very difficult works) for a mere song, simply in order to have cash in hand to meet my present difficulties. And for the same reason I am now composing some clavier sonatas."

The first two Prussian Quartets were written with an eye to pleasing Friedrich Wilhelm, without being too difficult for him.

In the Quartet in F Major, however, the royal violoncello was given a much larger part and made to establish its independence. This quartet, written as it was in one of the most tormented periods of Mozart's life, could never have been fashionable. It could only be exactly what it is — a complex, abstract, personal masterpiece, highly original in the boldness of its finale — and certainly too difficult for the King of Prussia to play.

Perhaps the real reason Mozart never completed the series of six quartets he was commissioned to write had simply to do with the fact that the Quartet in F Major incurred the King's displeasure.

It is one of the most daring of Mozart's ten major string quartets. It is certainly the most aggressive.

\*   \*   \*

**1. Allegro moderato**   The first subject states a question

287

which opens *piano*, and then, in brutal fashion, becomes *forte* in the second bar. A short affirmative answer is given and an urgent conversation follows between the first violin and the violoncello, thus leaving the second violin and the viola almost constantly in the shade. Despite the emphasis placed on the violoncello, the resonance of the quartet as a whole is perfectly balanced. After a short polyphonic development the movement ends with an exquisite and surprising little coda pulsing with emotion.

**2. Andante in C Major**   This *andante* (which is maked *allegretto* in some editions) is not a true slow movement. It is built entirely around one single, imperious and insistent rhythmic phrase. It is a solemn, dissonant song of melancholy bitterness.

**3. Minuet and trio**   The minuet is conventional enough, although the irregularity of its accentuation give it a somewhat uncertain gait. The trio is almost a perfect twin — although it is a little less sullen.

**4. Allegro**   This finale is remarkable on every count. It is certainly the most violent finale ever given by Mozart to a chamberwork. Its single turbulent theme leads to a breath-taking, fragmented development which calls for great virtuosity on the part of the four instrumentalists. A feverish, demonic rhythm pervades this allegro, which shows only too clearly the state of disorder in which Mozart found himself in June 1790. However, his mastery is supreme and the whole tone of the movement is entirely new. This, the last of Mozart's string quartets, is filled with dazzling promise.

**Works written between June and December 1790**

*Instrumentation of Handel's 'Alexander's Feast', K. 591*
*Instrumentation of Handel's 'Ode for St. Cecilia's Day',*
*K. 592*
*Orchestration of Benedikt Schachk's comical Duet 'Nun*
*liebes Weibchen', K. 625*

# 45

# 1790 | String Quintet in D Major, K. 593

1. **Larghetto; allegro**
2. **Adagio in G Major**
3. **Minuet and trio**
4. **Allegro**

Between January 26th, 1790, the date of the première of 'Cosi fan tutte' and June, Mozart managed to compose only two string quartets for the King of Prussia.

Between June and December he wrote nothing.

He started a Sonata in F Major for Princess Friederike, but it never got beyond the stage of three rough sketches.

These six months of silence are a clear indication of how grave was his crisis and how deep was his despair.

On August 14th he wrote to Michael Puchberg in absolute desperation:

"Dearest Friend and Brother, Whereas I felt tolerably well yesterday, I am absolutely wretched today. I could not sleep all night for pain. I must have got over-heated yesterday from walking so much and then without knowing it have caught a chill. Picture to yourself my condition — ill and consumed by worries and anxieties. Such a state quite definitely prevents me from recovering. In a week or a fortnight I shall be better off — certainly — but at present I am in want! Can you not help me out with a trifle? The *smallest* sum would be very welcome just now. You would, for the moment at least, bring peace of mind to your true friend, servant and brother, W. A. Mozart".

That same day, in these blackest hours of Mozart's life, Puchberg sent him ten florins — the smallest sum he had lent him so far. Despite his admiration for Mozart, it seems clear that Puchberg had come to regard him as little more than an insufferable sponger.

The double marriage of the Archdukes Franz and Ferdinand, the sons of Leopold II to the daughters of the King and Queen of Naples, in Vienna, was an excuse for all sorts of festivities — from which Mozart found himself excluded. There were performances of operas by Salieri and Weigl; but none of Mozart's were staged. He received no invitations. His former admirers could not possibly be unaware of his wretched plight; yet no one made any effort to help him.

Leopold II's coronation ceremony was to take place on October 9th, in Frankfurt. Although he was not included among the official guests of the Imperial Court, Mozart decided to go to Frankfurt nevertheless, in the vague hope of proving to the world that, at the age of thirty-four, he was not yet finished. But to get there, he needed money — and he had none. For the moment, and only out of charity, Puchberg would let him have only a few florins. However, Mozart succeeded in borrowing a sizable sum of money from one Heinrich Lackenbacher. The loan was to be repaid in two years' time. In addition, he managed to make an arrangement with the publisher Hoffmeister which put still more money in his pocket. He had never borrowed such large sums before and it was a source of worry to him throughout his trip.

Mozart did not go alone — his brother-in-law Franz Hofer went with him. The two men left Vienna on September 23, 1790.

Perhaps it had to do with the fact that he had left the city where he was being stifled — but suddenly Mozart felt almost joyful. He wrote to Constanze from Frankfurt am Main on September 28th.

"At Regensburg we lunched magnificently to the accompaniment of divine music, we had angelic cooking and some glorious Moselle wine ... I am firmly resolved to make as much money as I can here and then return to you with great joy. What a glorious life we shall have then! I will work — work so hard — that no unforeseen accidents shall ever reduce us to such desperate straits again."

Mozart's high spirits were doomed to last only a short while. At Frankfurt, he was welcomed with such enthusiasm that he decided to give a concert.

"Already I am being invited everywhere — and however tiresome it may be to let myself be on view, I see nevertheless how necessary it is."

A performance of 'Don Giovanni' was advertised in his honour but in the end, it was 'Figaro' that was actually played.

His concert was given on October 15th, from 11 a.m. to

2 p.m. The programme consisted entirely of his own works. Mozart himself played his Concerto in D Major, which he had written three years previously. Henceforth, it became known as the 'Coronation' Concerto.

On that same day, some Prince hosted a big *déjeuner* and the Hessian troops held their manoeuvres, so the audience at Mozart's concert was fairly thin and the revenues from it were disappointing.

"True, I am famous, admired and popular here; on the other hand, the Frankfurt people are even more stingy than the Viennese."

His trip brought him nowhere near the success he expected from it. He was extremely bitter about this, but it was too late for regrets.

"It was a splendid success from the point of view of honour and glory, but it was a failure as far as money was concerned."

He wrote again to Constanze the evening after his concert.

"I shall therefore leave on Monday. I must close this letter, or I shall miss the post. I gather from your letters that you have not yet received any from me from Frankfurt. Yet I sent you four. Moreover I seem to notice that you doubt my punctuality or rather my eagerness to write to you, and this pains me bitterly. Surely you ought to know me better. Good God! Only love me half as much as I love you, and I shall be content. Ever your Mozart."

Mozart left Frankfurt on October 16th, after a twenty-day stay. On his way home, he stopped at Offenbach to meet the publisher Johann André. At Mainz, he played for the

# 1790

Prince-Elector Karl Friedrich von Erthal for a miserable pittance. He reached Mannheim on the very day the town was having its first performance of his 'Marriage of Figaro'. On November 4th, he wrote to Constanze from Munich: "I only wanted to spend a day here; but now I am obliged to remain until the 5th or 6th, for the Elector has asked me to perform at a concert which he is giving for the King of Naples. It is greatly to the credit of the Viennese Court that the King has to hear me in a foreign country."

This was a sarcastic allusion to the fact that when King Ferdinand and Queen Caroline of Naples came to Vienna two months previously (for the marriage of their daughters) Mozart had not been asked to play for them.

A few days later Mozart was back in Vienna, in a better frame of mind.

While in Munich, Mozart met some old and very good friends from Mannheim. He also made some new Masonic friends. The warmth of their company renewed his gusto for life and restored his creative fire — to such an extent that over the next twelve months (which was to be the last year of his life) he wrote masterpiece after masterpiece. While he was away, Constanze moved back into town and had set up house in an apartment on the Rauhensteingasse. This was to be Mozart's final lodging.

A letter from O'Reilly, manager of the Italian Opera in London, was waiting for him when he returned. O'Reilly invited him to come to England and to write two operas for him for a very handsome sum, with an advance of 300 pounds sterling. However, Mozart was tied to Vienna by his duties as Court composer and, above all, by his debts. He had no option but to decline the invitation.

Meanwhile, the English impresario Salomon invited Joseph Haydn to give several concerts in London. Haydn accepted. Prince Esterhazy had recently died and left his Court composer and musician an annual pension of 1000 florin, as well as his liberty. Mozart was inconsolable, even though Salomon promised him that he would be the next to be invited.

On December 15th, he said goodbye to his beloved Haydn, with tears in his eyes. The two men never saw each other again.

A little later, in this same month of December, Mozart wrote his String Quintet in D Major, K. 593, for two violins, two violas and violoncello. This work was written for a wealthy Hungarian merchant, Johann Tost, an amateur violinist who had commissioned many quartets from Haydn.

Artaria's edition of 1793 carries this inscription: *"Composto per un amatore ungarese"*.

*     *     *

**1. Larghetto; allegro**   The movement opens with a slow introduction interrupted by solemn pauses, during which the violoncello enters into serious conversation with the other instruments. The *allegro* contains themes which are sometimes sprightly and playful, sometimes unsure and hesitant — but always elegant and decorative. The development is elaborate, dissonant and full of contrasting *pianos* and *fortes*. Before the recapitulation (a very unusual feature for the first movement of a piece of Mozart's chamber music) the initial *larghetto* reappears, with fine dramatic effect. Then, in the space of nine bars, Mozart's master hand picks up the *allegro* once again and brings the movement to an end with breath-taking speed. The scoring in this quintet (as in the next one, K. 614) is quite superb. The violoncello is accorded an importance which seems to indicate that Mozart was perhaps thinking of the violoncellist King of Prussia while writing it down. The addition of a second viola helps to liberate the violoncello and it gives the resonance of the ensemble a richness which cannot be equalled by a string quartet. The year 1790 was the least prolific of Mozart's entire life, but by the year's end he had not only recovered his creative force, he was also displaying an incomparable degree of zest in his composition.

**2. Adagio in G Major** Despite the clear, happy key of G Major, this thoughtful, passionate *adagio* is by no means free of a certain uneasiness. The first theme, interrupted by silences as in the *larghetto* of the first movement, has something overpowering about it. In the middle of the movement, a miracle occurs: it is as if Mozart were noting down messages from his secret soul. This extraordinary passage lies between Bars 52 and 56. Several things happen simultaneously: the ascending counterpoint of the first violin is balanced by descending trilled motifs from the second violin; and the violas move by intervals of seconds, against the fragmented pizzicato of the violoncello.

**3. Minuet and trio** This is one of Mozart's most vigorous minuets: it is noteworthy for its off-hand manner and canonic build-up. The trio is a very freely expressed, polished serenade. It too contains polyphonic elements and offers the listener the pizzicatos which Mozart so seldom uses.

**4. Allegro** The imposing polyphonic structure of this finale entitles it to be classed with the finale of the 'Jupiter' Symphony. After the exposition of a theme in 6/8 time, which at first seems tame but which is actually very vivacious, the counterpoint becomes more tightly knit, and the instruments compete with one another in virtuosity at a break-neck pace. The dash and dynamism they display here are irresistible. The score is written with incomparable skill and grace, with delicate touches of humour here and there.

**Sole work composed by Mozart in December 1790**

*Fantasia for a mechanical organ in F Minor, No. 1, K. 594*

# 46

# 1791

# Concerto for piano and orchestra in B Flat Major, No. 27, K. 595

1. **Allegro**
2. **Larghetto in E Flat Major**
3. **Allegro**

On January 5th, 1791, Mozart noted the composition of his last piano concerto in his thematic catalogue: the Concerto in B Flat Major, No. 27, K. 595. We do not know for whom this piece was intended — possibly for a student, because he gave it two cadenzas. Perhaps it was for the twenty-five year-old Franz Xaver Süssmayr, who was his new composition pupil. Perhaps he hoped to play it himself one day. However, it is clear that Mozart was back at work with renewed enthusiasm. (He felt encouraged by the novelty and the general excellence of the string quintet he had recently completed.) It was time to rid himself of all gloomy thoughts, to be happy at all costs and to make a lot of money — for Constanze was pregnant for the sixth time, with the baby due in July.

As soon as his concerto was finished, Mozart set to work writing the dance music for the Carnival, which was one of the duties of his appointment. During January, February and March, he composed at least a dozen minuets, thirteen German dances, nine contredanses and six ländler. These dances are pure gems. The melodic inventiveness and especially the richness of the orchestration of the six Minuets K. 599, for example, make them something absolutely unique in the whole of Mozart's instrumental work.

Mozart was in no position to turn down commissions and he had agreed to write several fantasias for mechanical organ for a certain Count Deym, who owned a wax museum. Mozart disliked this instrument, which sounded nothing like a true organ, and which — in Mozart's own words — consisted solely of little pipes which sounded too high-pitched and too childish for his taste. Mozart was always honest, however, and he took considerable care over this work. The Fantasias in F Minor, K. 594 and K. 608, together with an 'Adagio' in F Major, K. 616, constitute the sum total of Mozart's organ music — with the exception of seventeen short church sonatas which he wrote in Salzburg.

Like the String Quartet in D Major, K. 499, the Piano Concerto in B Flat Major is one of a kind, written in a new style lacking the heat and vigour of the great concertos that preceded it. It is graceful and serene, and strictly classical in form.

\* \* \*

**1. Allegro**   A movement remarkable for its charm and gentleness, free of all tension. One can only admire the pure beauty of its lyricism, the depth of its expression and the perfect balance of its sonority. The admirable sparseness of style is one of the characteristics of Mozart's last works.

**2. Larghetto in E Flat Major**   This simple, tender *rêverie* is one of the most poetic of Mozart's slow movements. Here we have art at its most refined: only the very essence of the music is retained. The coda contains a short moment of barely discernible excitement.

**3. Allegro**   A sprightly finale, although its gaiety is toned down somewhat by several modulations in the minor key. Nine days after writing this rondo, Mozart used its main theme in a *lied* written in a popular vein: "Sehnsucht nach dem Frühlinge", K. 596. During this period, when he was composing so many German dances, minuets and contredanses, Mozart was steeped in folk-music: a listener will note many examples of this in 'The Magic Flute'.

**Works written between January 5th and April 12th, 1791**

*Lieder:*
  *'Sehnsucht nach dem Frühlinge', K. 596*
  *'Im Frühlingsanfang', K. 597*
  *'Das Kinderspiel', K. 598*
*Six Minuets for orchestra, K. 599*
*Six German Dances for Orchestra, K. 600*
*Four Minuets for orchestra, K. 601*

*Four German Dances for orchestra, K. 602*
*Two Contredanses for orchestra, K. 603*
*Two Minuets for orchestra, K. 604*
*Three German Dances for orchestra, K. 605*
*Six Ländler for orchestra, K. 606*
*Contredanse for orchestra, K. 607*
*Fantasia for a mechanical organ in F Minor, No. 2, K. 608*
*Five Contredanses for orchestra, K. 609*
*Contredanse for orchestra, K. 610 ('Les Filles malicieuses')*
*German Dance, K. 611*
*Aria for bass 'Per questa bella mano', K. 612*
*Piano Variations in F Major, K. 613*

# 47

# String Quintet in E Flat Major, K. 614

1. Allegro di molto
2. Andante in B Flat Major
3. Minuet and trio
4. Allegro

On March 4th, a clarinettist by the name of Joseph Bähr invited Mozart and his sister-in-law Aloysia Lange to take part in his concert. Mozart seized the opportunity to play his Concerto in B Flat Major which he had written in January.

About this time he also received the first of four commissions he obtained during this last year of his life, which was to prove a most prolific time. The Manager of the Auf der Wieden Theatre, Emmanuel Schikaneder, was an artist whom Mozart had known for a long time, as well as a fellow-Mason with whom he was very friendly. Schikaneder's main interests lay in the fields of *singspiel* and fairy-plays. At that time, Schikaneder's theatre was in competition with a theatre in the Leopoldstadt quarter, directed by a man called Marinelli. Schikaneder had no intention of being driven to the wall and came up with an idea for a fairy-play, drawn from a tale of the East by Liebeskind: 'Lulu, oder die Zauberflöte' ('Lulu, or The Magic Flute'). Schikaneder had written an original libretto, entitled 'The Magic Flute' which he offered to Mozart. Mozart was never so happy as when he was writing for the theatre. Thus he accepted Schikaneder's suggestion without hesitation, even though fairy-plays represented something entirely new to him.

We shall see before long how 'The Magic Flute' was changed from its original concept as a simple fairy-play, and how it became a Masonic opera.

On April 12th, Mozart finished his Quintet in E Flat Major, K. 614, the most original of his seven string quintets.

\* \* \*

**1. Allegro di molto**   The first subject recalls the opening theme of 'The Hunt' Quartet, K. 458 — which is also a gay, sprightly piece of music. This theme, embellished with three trills, dominates this lively movement in which the spirit of the Haydn Quartets lives again. The five instruments converse among themselves with unquenchable ardour. When the development begins, the first violin cannot contain itself: twice, it produces sounds which for all the world are actual cries of joy (Bars 90 to 96, and 100 to 106). The scoring is complex, but light, and Mozart shows through it his powers of invention and incomparably rich imagination.

**2. Andante in B Flat Major**   This marvellous *andante*, replete with a deep and solemn joy, is a sort of 'theme and variations'. It begins rather like the *romanze* in the Serenade 'Eine Kleine Nachtmusik'. The single theme becomes more richly ornamented with each repetition. There are sequences of markedly dissonant modulations.

**3. Minuet and trio**   This is perhaps the most vigorous, the most virile, of Mozart's minuets. It is certainly the most animated. The trio is a twin brother to the third of the German Dances, K. 602; both of them imitate a barrel-organ.

**4. Allegro**   During the second episode of this rondo, Mozart transforms the frivolous theme in a most fantastic way, giving the entire episode the contrapuntal depth of a solid sonata-type development. He also shows his enormous virtuosity and biting wit.

**Works written between April 12th**
**and June 18th, 1791**

*Chorus 'Viviamo felici', K. 615 (lost)*
*Andante for a small mechanical organ in F Major, K. 616*
*Adagio in C Minor and Rondo in C Major for glass harmonica, flute, oboe, viola and violoncello, K. 617*
*Adagio for glass harmonica in A Major, K. 356*

# 48
## Motet 'Ave verum, corpus', K. 618

**1791**

At the beginning of May, Mozart addressed a petition to the municipal councillors of Vienna, asking to be appointed to succeed *Kapellmeister* Hoffman, who was old and ailing. As he wished, he was granted the unpaid position of Assistant *Kapellmeister* at St. Stephen's Cathedral, on May 9th: but Hoffman outlived his new assistant.

About this time Mozart wrote two very beautiful works for a young blind musician, Marianne Kirchgessner, who was a virtuoso on the glass harmonica. These works, which made her famous, were an 'Adagio and Rondo' for glass harmonica, flute, oboe, viola, and violoncello, K. 617, and a short 'Adagio' K. 356, in C Major.

Constanze did not have an easy pregnancy and again had to go to Baden. Mozart had much to do in Vienna, which made it easier for him to reconcile himself to being separated from his wife and little Karl — who was now almost seven. Besides, Baden was not so far away and Mozart managed to spend a few hours with his family every now and then.

He wrote to a friend, Anton Stoll, choirmaster of Baden, and asked him to find accommodation for his wife and son. He was in gay spirits, and started off his letter with this greeting:

"Dear Old Stoll! Don't be a poll! Will you please find a small apartment for my wife? She only needs two rooms, or one room and a dressing-room. But the main thing is that they should be on the ground floor.... I should like to know whether the theatre in Baden is open yet— Please reply as quickly as possible ... This is the silliest letter I have ever written in my life; but it is just the very thing for you."

Constanze and Karl left for Baden at the beginning of June and Mozart reorganized his life on a bachelor footing. As an economy measure, he discharged their maid, Leonora. He accepted every invitation he received, dining with Puchberg or Schikaneder, sleeping at the Leutgebs' and between compositions he wrote to Constanze.

On June 6th, he wrote the following letter to Constanze (whom he had nick-named affectionately 'Stanzi-Marini'), in his faulty French:

*"Ma très cher Epouse! J'écris cette lettre dans la petite chambre au jardin chez Leutgeb ou j'ai couché cette nuit excellement — et j'espere que ma chere epouse aura passée cette nuit aussi bien que moi. J'y passerai cette nuit aussi, puisque j'ai congédié Leonore et je serais tout seul à la maison, ce qui n'est pas agreable.*

*J'attends avec beaucoup d'impatience une lettre qui m'apprendra comme vous avés passé le jour d'hier. Je tremble*

*quand je pense au bain de Saint Antoin, car je crains tou-*
*jours le risque de tomber sur l'escalier en sortant — et je*
*me trouve entre l'esperance et la crainte — une situation*
*bien desagreable! Si vous n'etiés pas grosse, je craignerais*
*moins. Mais abandonnons cette idée triste! Le ciel aura*
*certainement soin de ma chère Stanzi-Marini."*

Two days later he visited Baden but he had to keep his
visit short in order to return to Vienna to attend a concert
by Marianne Kirchgessner. Much to his disappointment,
the concert was put off until June 19th.

*"Criés avec moi contre mon mauvais sort!",* he wrote
immediately to Constanze. *"Mlle Kirchgessner ne*
*donne pas son academie lundi! Par conséquent j'aurais*
*pu vous posseder, ma chère, tout ce jour de dimanche . . ."*

Then he added — this time in German: "I cannot tell you
what I would not give to be with you at Baden instead of
being stuck here. From sheer boredom I composed today
an aria for my opera. I got up as early as half past four."

On June 12th, in the midst of his work on 'The Magic
Flute', Mozart went to Marinelli's theatre (Schikaneder's
rival) to attend a performance of a fairy-play by Wenzel
Müller titled 'Kaspar der Faggotist, oder die Zauberzither'
('Caspar the Bassoonist, or The Magic Zither'). Its plot
bore a rather too close resemblance to that of 'The Magic
Flute'. It was probably because of his discovery that
Mozart managed to persuade Schikaneder to change his
libretto into an apotheosis of Freemasonry.

Mozart did not like living alone. Constanze did not write
to him as often as he would have liked and he worried

about her. To fight his loneliness he would go to the theatre or have supper in a restaurant; then he would hurry home and write to his wife, urging her not to go to the Casino, where everyone would notice her — besides which, she would not even be able to dance because of her condition. In the end he managed to spend six whole days in Baden. On one of his visits Mozart again met Anton Stoll, who was always ready to lend a helping hand. It turned out that Stoll had recently had Mozart's Mass in C Major, K. 371 (known as the 'Coronation' Mass) sung in his church in Baden. To thank him for having found an apartment for Constanze, and for looking after her during her husband's absence, Mozart offered him, for use on Corpus Christi Day, the celebrated motet 'Ave verum corpus' which was completed on June 18th. Mozart had written no church music since his Mass in C Minor, which he composed in 1782-1783.

\* \* \*

The 'Ave verum corpus' is a motet in D Major, for four voices, with accompaniment from strings and organ. An indefinable charm radiates from the four yellowed pages on which Mozart noted the forty-six bars of the piece in a delicate hand and without a single mistake.

This polyphonic composition, so perfectly balanced and spaced out, moves along in a series of slow modulations with infinite grace and naturalness. These pages exude an aura of sincere piety and deep emotion.

The stylistic beauty and the harmonic colouring of this work will put the listener in mind of the priests' chorus in 'The Magic Flute': 'O, Isis und Osiris' (No. 18 in the score).

## Works written between June 18th and September 30th, 1791

*Masonic Cantata 'Dir, Seele des Weltalls', K. 429*
*Opera seria 'La Clemenza di Tito', K. 621*

# 49

## 1791 | 'Die Zauberflöte', K. 620 (The Magic Flute)

One of the most amusing stories concerning the composition of 'The Magic Flute' has to do with Schikaneder locking Mozart up in a small wooden pavilion in the garden of the Auf der Wieden Theatre and plying him with delicious food to help the work along. If any of the tales are to be believed, Mozart had a high old time there in the company of the actors (and actresses) in Schikaneder's troupe.

This same pavilion can be seen today in the garden of the Mozarteum, in Salzburg.

Money worries continued to plague Mozart so much that at the beginning of July he again had to borrow from Puchberg in order to pay for Constanze's apartment in Baden.

In a letter to his wife dated July 5th, he complained of being tired.

*Papageno, the bird-catcher in 'The Magic Flute'. Illustration from the first edition of the libretto.*

## 'Die Zauberflöte', K. 620

"I hope to hold you in my arms on Saturday, perhaps sooner. As soon as my business here is over, I shall be with you, for I mean to take a long rest in your arms; and indeed I shall need it, for this mental worry and anxiety and all the running about connected with it is really exhausting me."

On the 7th, the wrote again.

"You cannot imagine how I have been aching for you all this long while. I can't describe what I have been feeling — a kind of emptiness, which hurts me dreadfully — a kind of longing, which is never satisfied, which never ceases, and which persists, nay rather increases daily. When I think how merry we were together at Baden like children — and what sad, weary hours I am spending here! Even my work gives me no pleasure, because I am accustomed to stop working now and then and exchange a few words with you. Alas! this pleasure is no longer possible. If I go to the piano and sing something out of my opera, I have to stop at once, for this stirs my emotions too deeply. Basta!"

Nervous, in poor health, and suffering from the separation from his loved ones, Mozart wrote to Constanze nearly every day. These letters contain many friendly greetings and little jokes, intended for his pupil Süssmayr, whom he nicknamed Snai or Sauermayer, and who was lucky enough, he, to be in Baden.

On July 11th, Mozart brought his family back to Vienna. On the 26th, Constanze gave birth to a son Franz Xaver Wolfgang Amadeus. He and his elder brother Karl were the only ones of Mozart's six children to live to maturity.

At the end of July, Mozart received a visit from a stranger, who brought him a commission for a *Requiem*. This man (though Mozart, of course, did not know it) was the servant of a certain Count Walsegg-Stuppach, a musician of no talent who used to buy works anonymously from known composers and then pass them off as his own. His wife had just died and he wanted Mozart to compose for him a Mass for the Dead.

In his current state of nervousness and tension, Mozart could not help but be impressed by this mysterious visit. He accepted the commission, for by now 'The Magic Flute' was very nearly finished (but not completely, even though he had already entered it in his thematic catalogue).

He then received a third commission, this time for an *opera seria* in two acts, which the theatrical company of Prague wished to stage in that city on the occasion of Leopold II's coronation as King of Bohemia. He was to work to an old libretto by Metastasio, 'La Clemenza di Tito', and was allowed only three weeks for the composition. The whole project seemed unrealizable. However, the pay offered for this enterprise was so attractive that in spite of his excessive work-load and the poor state of his health, Mozart laid aside the 'Requiem' he had just sketched out, and settled down to this new task. There was not a moment to spare . . .

Karl and the baby were boarded out and Mozart left for Prague with Constanze. He took Süssmayr with him: he could save time by having his pupil help him write the recitatives. The clarinettist Anton Stadler was to join them later in Prague to play the solos which Mozart had arranged for him in the two arias: 'Parto, parto', with clarinet obbligato (No. 9); and the rondo 'Non piu fiori', with basset horn obbligato (No. 23).

As Mozart was about ready to leave for Prague, the mysterious stranger appeared again, and demanded the score for the 'Requiem'. Mozart was very embarrassed, and tried to explain how he had felt compelled to accept the commission from Prague; he asked his visitor to be kind enough to give him an extension of time.

As might be expected, he worked without a break during the trip, so much so that when he arrived at the Duscheks, at the Bertramka, he collapsed from exhaustion. He was at the end of his tether and he wondered anxiously if he could manage to hold out. However, he had to attend a reception given in his honour by one of the Prague Masonic Lodges and on top of it all, right in the midst of feverish last-minute arrangements for his new opera, he had to direct a performance of 'Don Giovanni' (on September 2nd) which was attended by Leopold II and his Court.

None dared suggest to Mozart that he take a rest: 'La Clemenza di Tito' simply could not be produced without him.

As planned, the opera had its debut on the evening of the coronation, September 6th. The cost to Mozart was three weeks of extremely concentrated and exhausting effort. The grandiose and sombre *opera seria* 'La Clemenza di Tito' betrays the haste with which it was composed. Metastasio's dull libretto failed to arouse Mozart's interest. In any event, the work was not very successful. The

Empress described it as German *porcheria*; the papers never even mentioned it.

At this point Mozart's health began to deteriorate rapidly. After the production of 'La Clemenza di Tito', his fatigue and disappointment combined to plunge him into a deep melancholy. Everyone begged him to take a few days' rest but the première of 'The Magic Flute' was scheduled for the end of September, and once again he had to be off.

Mozart returned to Vienna sick at heart. He was terribly worried about his health. He knew that he ought to stop; but it was absolutely impossible for him to do so. He simply had to attend to the final arrangements for his German opera.

On September 28th, he noted the composition of the overture to 'The Magic Flute' in his thematic catalogue along with that of the 'March of the Priests' (No. 9) which serves as the overture to the second act. This was not the first time Mozart had written the overture to a dramatic work last of all. He was, however, breaking new ground by giving the second act of his last opera an instrumental prelude.

The dress rehearsal was finally held on September 29th; the première took place on the 30th.

The audience which crowded into the foyer of the Auf der Wieden Theatre that evening was clearly not the Viennese public who had applauded Mozart's great successes in former days. They came from an unpretentious suburb and they were faithful in their support of their local theatre, as people still are to this day. They came to hear 'The Magic Flute' not because the music was by Mozart, but because the play was the work of the famous Schikaneder. The cast was not particularly brilliant. In fact, Schikaneder was probably the only well-known actor in the company. Benedikt Schack sang Tamino and Marianne Gottlieb (the original Barbarina in 'The Marriage of Figaro') played the part of Pamina. The Queen of the Night was sung by Josepha Hofer, Mozart's sister-in-law.

Pale, tense, and nervous, Mozart conducted the opera from his harpsichord, while Süssmayr turned the pages of the score.

At first the audience seemed baffled by this fairy-play, full of Egyptian symbols, which unrolled to the strains of a music that was too clever and too beautiful for them. There was no reaction during the first act and Mozart shuddered at the thought that the failure of 'La Clemenza di Tito' was about to be repeated.

Suddenly, during the second act, the audience began to enjoy themselves quite openly: they started applauding each number with growing enthusiasm.

Mozart could hardly believe his own ears.

At the end of the performance, this simple audience shouted for him so insistently that he was overcome with emotion and he hid himself in the wings. Schikaneder and Süssmayr, beside themselves with delight, had to drag him on stage to bow to the audience and acknowledge their applause.

Slowly the news that 'The Magic Flute' had been well

received spread throughout Vienna and its success was repeated night after night. The opera enjoyed twenty-four sell-out performances in October. Naturally, the money Mozart made from this unexpected success gave him temporary relief from his perpetual financial crisis.

For Schikaneder himself, Mozart wrote several songs in a popular style; they brought him a stupendous success. The role of Papageno is a magnificient part for an actor who is loved by his public (and who is also a bit of a ham, as Schikaneder undoubtedly was) to show himself to his best advantage. The result is therefore predictable; every night, Schikaneder scored a triumph, and received an ovation from the audience.

Three days after the first performance, Mozart handed over direction of the orchestra to the theatre's regular conductor. Constanze had returned to Baden after the première of the opera, with the baby, her sister Sophie Haibel, and Süssmayr. Once again, he was alone in Vienna.

The correspondence between Mozart and his wife resumed. In a letter written on October 8th and 9th, Mozart related an incident which he found amusing and which had taken place in the theatre.

". . . During Papageno's aria with the glockenspiel I went behind the scenes, as I felt a sort of impulse today to play it myself. Well, just for fun, at the point where Schikaneder has a pause, I played an arpeggio. He was startled, looked behind the wings and saw me. When he had his next pause, I played no arpeggio. This time he stopped and refused to go on. I guessed what he was thinking and again played a chord. He then struck the glockenspiel and said *'shut up'*. Whereupon everyone laughed. I am inclined to think that this joke taught many of the audience for the first time that Papageno does not play the instrument himself. By the way, you have no idea how charming the music sounds when you hear it from a box close to the orchestra — it sounds much better than from the gallery. As soon as you return — you must try this for yourself . . . Farewell, my love — I kiss you millions of times and am ever your . . . Mozart.

P.S. — Kiss Sophie for me. I send Süssmayr a few good *nose-pulls* and a proper *hair-tug* and Stoll a thousand greetings. Adieu. The hour is striking — Farewell — We shall meet again.''

Then, after these words of farewell borrowed from Sarastro ('Die Stunde Schlägt, wir sehn uns wieder') Mozart tells his wife, in a second postscript, that he has hunted everywhere in vain for two pairs of yellow winter trousers, which she must have inadvertently sent with the boots that go with them to the laundry.

At first sight, the libretto of 'The Magic Flute' appears to be little more than a childish, rather absurd fairy-story. It is full of Masonic symbols which are of no interest to us today. However, we cannot completely ignore them, for they meant a great deal to Mozart and to Schikaneder. Goethe readily understood their significance and he found the libretto so interesting that he seriously considered writing a sequel to it.

The Masonic symbolism in 'The Magic Flute' must also have been recognized by the Freemasons of many countries who used Mozart's ritual music during their ceremonies. As originally written, the libretto told the story of a good fairy, a wicked sorcerer, and a pair of lovers who must submit to all sorts of tests before they are finally united. (Obviously, certain incongruous elements exist in the final version as a result of oversight and "spill-over" from the original version — as for example the surprising stage direction requiring the young Prince Tamino, about to be initiated into the mysteries of Isis and Osiris, to wear a 'magnificent Japanese hunting costume'.)

In mid-June 1791, Mozart and Schikaneder reversed the situation and in the end it is Pamina, daughter of the Queen of the Night (who symbolizes Evil), who is spirited away by Sarastro, priest of the mysteries of Isis and Osiris (who symbolizes Good). (The name Sarastro recalls that of Zoroaster, the reformer of the ancient Persian religion, who later became Nietzsche's Zarathustra, the prototype of his Superman.)

Schikaneder was a Freemason and he found Mozart's suggestions highly interesting. He agreed to the proposed changes, provided that his own role as Papageno the bird-catcher (his only real contribution to the scenario) did not suffer. Thus, from the simple fairy-play it was originally, 'The Magic Flute' became an opera in which magic and comic elements blend with Masonic philosophy.

Mozart, the master of so many different music-forms, died before he had an opportunity to make the style of German opera perfect. 'The Magic Flute' consequently shows signs of widely different influences.

The work is primarily a German opera aimed at a broad

public. Accordingly, Mozart turned certain numbers intended for Papageno into typical German popular songs: his first song, in couplets, 'Der Vogelfänger bin ich, ja' (No. 2); the duet 'Bei Mannern, welche Liebe fühlen' (No. 7), which he sings with Pamina, and which Mozart called 'Mann und Weib'; and the aria in three couplets (with three different *glockenspiel* accompaniments) 'Ein Mädchen oder Weibchen' (No. 20) — (during which Mozart played his little trick on Schikaneder).

Traces of popular music can also be detected in Papageno's 'Schön Mädchen, jung und fein' (in No. 6), as well as in 'Wer viel wagt' (finale of the first act), and 'Klinget, Glöckenspiel' (finale of the second act), both of which are sung by Papageno.

Sarastro's solemn aria 'In diesen heil'gen Hallen'(No. 15) is also a beautiful German song.

The influence of *opera buffa* can be seen mainly in Monostatos' song 'Ha, hab'ich euch noch erwischt' (finale I); the quintet — Tamino, Papageno, and the three Ladies — ' Wie? Wie? Wie? ' (No. 12); and Monostatos' charming little aria 'Alles fühlt der Liebe Freuden' (No. 13).

The Queen of the Night's two coloratura arias, 'O Zitt're nicht, mein lieber Sohn' (No. 4), and 'Der Hölle Rache kocht' (No. 14) both stem from *opera seria* and from *opera buffa*. In the first of these, the Queen is required to perform the most redoubtable feats of vocal agility through fourteen bars on the word 'dann' — 154 notes in all — ending in a perilous high F. This, of course, represents the lament of a loving mother whose beloved daughter has been torn from her side. In the second aria, the distraught mother has become a diabolical fury demanding vengeance of the cruelest nature.

The aria 'Dies Bildnis ist bezaubernd schön' (No. 3), in which Tamino expresses his love at first sight when he discovers Pamina's portrait, is the first true love song that Mozart wrote in an opera, since 'The Abduction from the Seraglio'. The outpourings of Ottavio, Guglielmo, and Ferrando pale into insignificance beside it.

In the finale of the first act, Tamino sings another beautiful aria while accompanying himself on his magic flute: 'Wie stark ist nicht dein Zauberton', which precedes his mysterious and gripping conversation with a priest and the chorus, 'Die Weisheitslehre dieser Knaben'.

Mozart gave Pamina a superb aria: 'Ach, ich fühl's' (No. 17). Written in G Minor and including chromatic effects which impart an anguished tone, it expresses a very real human grief with deep emotion.

Sarastro's aria with chorus, 'O, Isis und Osiris' (No. 10) and the priests' chorus 'O, Isis und Osiris, welche Wonne' (No. 18) — (which is so like the 'Ave verum corpus') are both in the style of Mozart's new ritual and Masonic music.

During the finale of the second act, without warning, Mozart slips in one of the most astonishing pieces of the whole opera: the disturbing C Minor chorale for the two men in armour, 'Der, welcher wandert diese Strasse', inspired by the German chorale 'Acht Gott, vom Himmel sieh'darein'. It is funerary music, which plunges us momentarily into black drama.

The quintet — sung by Monostatos, the Queen of the Night,

and the three Ladies in the second finale—'Nur stille, stille, stille,' *(moderato)* at the end of which these characters are engulfed in eternal night, is also highly unusual and is charged with unquestionable dramatic elements.

'The Magic Flute' is the one opera by Mozart which contains the greatest number of ensembles: for nine arias, there are two duets, four trios, two quintets, one chorus and two finales. It is also the opera in which he makes the fullest use of choral singing.

The two finales follow Lorenzo da Ponte's ideal, and are themselves truly operas in miniature: the first (No. 6) comprises nine parts; the second (No. 21) thirteen.

The work comes to an end with the solemn chorus 'Heil sei euch Geweihten', chanted to the glory of Isis and Osiris, followed by a second chorus 'Es siegte die Stärke', which is less imposing and more joyful — almost carefree as it proclaims the triple victory of Strength, of Beauty, and Wisdom.

The number three, the number of the Masonic triad, appears almost continuously throughout this work. The opera also begins and ends in the key of E Flat Major (which has three flats). The famous overture begins with three imposing chords. Nor should one overlook the three slaves of Sarastro; the three Ladies who impose three punishments on Papageno; the three Genii who counsel Tamino to show Constancy, Tolerance, and Discretion, in the regions ruled by Wisdom, Work, and Art; the three temples of Nature, Reason, and Wisdom; the ordeals by fire, by air, and by water; and many other examples . . .

In short, the symbolic significance of 'The Magic Flute' is so complicated that the initial success of the opera can only have been based on the beauty of the music and the splendour of the ensembles (and perhaps a little on Schikaneder's buffooneries).

# 50

**1791** | *Concerto for clarinet and orchestra in A Major, K. 622*

1. **Allegro**
2. **Adagio in D Major**
3. **Allegro**

"I have this moment returned from the opera", wrote Mozart to his wife in a letter started on October 7th and finished on the 8th, ". . . which was as full as ever. As usual the duet 'Mann und Weib' and Papageno's glockenspiel in Act I had to be repeated and also the trio of the boys in Act II. But what always gives me most pleasure is the *silent approval!* You can see how this opera is becoming more and more esteemed. Now for an account of my own doings. Immediately after your departure I played two games of billiards with Herr von Mozart, the fellow who wrote the opera which is running at Schikaneder's theatre; then I sold my nag for fourteen ducats; then I told Joseph to get Primus to fetch me some black coffee, with which I smoked a splendid pipe of

*Mozart, aged 32. Wax medallion by
Leonhard Posch, Vienna, 1788.*

tobacco; and then I orchestrated almost the whole of Stadler's rondo. Meanwhile I have had a letter which Stadler has sent me from Prague. All the Duscheks are well."

'Stadler's rondo', referred to by Mozart was the finale of the Clarinet Concerto in A Major, which had been finished on October 7th and was intended for Stadler. Mozart had composed it from a rough draft of a basset horn concerto he had sketched out (which he later abandoned) when he was writing his Clarinet Quintet in A Major, K. 581.

This is the only reference Mozart ever made in his writings to this concerto which is undeniably the most beautiful and perfect of all his concertos not intended for the piano. It is also his last great work.

\* \* \*

**1. Allegro**  This movement, which Mozart endowed with majestic proportions, contains no polyphonic display: it remains from start to finish a divertimento of the highest quality. The sparseness and the ingenuity of the initial theme reminds the listener of the first subject of the Piano Concerto in B Flat Major, K. 595. The music is peaceful and unobtrusive — at times, perhaps even a little haughty. Although the clarinet is shown to favourable advantage at all times, it is never allowed any form of exhibitionism. It seems to delight mainly in displaying the variety of its colouring, the wide compass of its register and the ease with which it can quickly move from the lowest to the highest notes.

**2. Adagio in D Major**   This movement is written in the free style of a fantasia. Slowly and solemnly, it unwinds for our pleasure a long cantilena of sedate beauty. The mood is that of a serene meditation. One must admire the exquisite transparency of the scoring.

**3. Allegro**   In this elegant final rondo, the dignified clarinet refuses to give way to buffoonery — as doubtless a bassoon would have done. Despite its playful mood, it retains its composure throughout. The music is neither gay nor sad.

*       *       *

On October 13th, in the company of his brother-in-law Hofer, Mozart went to fetch his son Karl from a school in Perchtoldsdorf, on the outskirts of Vienna. That evening, he took Salieri and Caterina Cavalieri to the Auf der Wieden Theatre to hear 'The Magic Flute'. Karl and his Grandmother Weber went along as well. The next day, Mozart hastened to tell his wife how Salieri and Mme Cavalieri had reacted to the opera. "You can hardly imagine how charming they were and how much they liked not only my music, but the libretto and everything. They both said that it was an *operone*, worthy to be performed for the grandest festival and before the greatest monarch, and that they would often go to see it, as they had never seen a more beautiful or delightful show. Salieri listened and watched most attentively and from the overture to the last chorus there was not a single number that did not call forth from him a bravo! or bello! . . . When it was over I drove

them home and then had supper at Hofer's with Karl . . .
Karl was absolutely delighted at being taken to the opera.
He is looking splendid. As far as health is concerned, he
could not be in a better place, but everything else there is
wretched, alas! . . . On the whole, Karl is no worse; but
at the same time he is not one whit better than he was.
He still has his old bad manners; he never stops chattering
just as he used to do in the past; and he is, if anything _less
inclined to learn than before,_ for out there (at Perchtoldsdorf) all he does is to wander about in the garden for five
hours in the morning and five hours in the afternoon, as
he has himself confessed. In short, the children do nothing
but eat, drink, sleep and go for walks . . . Yesterday the
whole day was taken up with that trip to Bernstorf, so I
could not write to you. But that you have not written to
me for two days, is really unforgivable. I hope that I shall
certainly have a letter from you today, and that tomorrow
I shall talk to you and embrace you with all my heart.
Farewell. Ever your Mozart."

Mozart ended the last letter he ever wrote with criticisms
concerning his son's education, and reproaches to his wife.
On October 15th, Mozart was in Baden. On the 16th, he
returned to Vienna with Sophie, Constanze and little Franz
Xaver. The two women were struck at how sick he looked.
From then on, Mozart's health became a constant source of
worry to those around him. Moreover, he cannot have had
many illusions about his condition himself.

However, he set to work again on the Requiem in D Minor,
K. 626. Only the Introit was ever completely finished:

the 'Requiem aeternam', and the 'Kyrie eleison'. He produced rough drafts for several sections and he sketched out eight bars of a sublime idea for a 'Lacrimosa'. Later, Süssmayr completed these rough drafts and he composed a 'Sanctus' and an 'Agnus Dei', imitating his master's style to the best of his ability.

During the night of November 20th, Mozart suddenly fell very ill. Constanze sent for Dr. Closset immediately. Mozart was suffering from partial paralysis and his hands and feet were swollen. Constanze and Sophie took turns watching by his bedside. Sophie and her mother, old Frau Weber, made a dressing-gown for the invalid to wear during his convalescence.

Mozart knew that he was dying and he did not bother to hide the fact from his family. He regretted that he would have to leave the 'Requiem' unfinished. Benedikt Schack reported that a rehearsal of the first portions of this Mass had been arranged for the afternoon of December 3rd, in Mozart's apartment.

Each evening, Mozart, in his imagination, attended the performance of 'The Magic Flute' which was continuing to draw full houses at Schikaneder's theatre.

On the day before his death, December 4th, he hummed Papageno's 'Der Vogelfänger bin ich, ja' in a feeble voice. A friend who happened to be visiting him at the time, *Kapellmeister* Roser, went to the piano and sang the song for him. Mozart laughed and wept at the same time.

Süssmayr stayed by his master's bedside. The 'Requiem' was spread out on the eiderdown and Mozart explained to the young man how he should finish it after his death.

That evening, Mozart appeared to be so close to death that the distraught Constanze sent Sophie to fetch a priest. The reverend gentleman required much pressing before he would agree to come.

They searched desperately for Dr. Closset. He was at the theatre and was not located until late that night. Mozart's forehead burned with fever. The doctor prescribed cold compresses, but these merely caused the patient to lose consciousness.

At midnight, Mozart turned his face to the wall and appeared to sleep. He died at 5 minutes to 1 a.m. on December 5th, 1791.

The next day a short religious service, without music, was held for him at St. Stephen's Cathedral. Constanze was too worn out and unwell to attend the ceremony, but Süssmayr was there, as well as Hofer, Sophie and her future husband Jakob Haibel (the composer), Schikaneder, Salieri and Baron van Swieten.

At this point there are conflicting stories. One story goes that because of the dreadful weather, the funeral procession dispersed before reaching St. Marx Cemetery and that the coffin was buried in a common grave with the paupers who had died over the previous few days.

On the other hand, there are stories which say the day was mild and humid. It remains that, to this day, the actual site of his grave is unknown.

# Bibliography

ANDERSON, Emily: *The Letters of Mozart and his family,* St. Martin's Press, New York, 1966.

BLOM, Eric: *Mozart,* Pellegrini and Cudaby Inc., New York, 1949.

DENT, J. Edward: *Mozart's Operas,* Oxford University Press, 1966.

EINSTEIN, Alfred: *Mozart, l'homme et l'oeuvre,* Desclée de Brouwer, 1954.

GIRDLESTONE, Cuthbert: *Mozart and his Piano Concertos,* Dover Publications, New York, 1964.

HUGHES, Rosemary: *Haydn,* Pellegrini and Cudaby Inc., New York, 1950.

JAHN, Otto: *Life of Mozart,* Cooper Square Publishers Inc., New York, 1970.

KELLY, Michael: *Reminiscences,* London, 1826.

KÖCHEL, Ludwig von: *Chronolgisch-thematisches Verzeichnis sämtlicher Tonwerke Wolfgang Amade Mozarts,* Leipzig, 1937.

LANDON, H. C. Robbins: *The Mozart Companion,* in collaboration with Donald Mitchell, Faber and Faber, London, 1956.

MASSIN, Jean and Brigitte: *Wolfgang Amadeus Mozart,* Club Français du Livre, Paris, 1959.

NEWMAN, Ernest: *Great Operas,* Vintage Books, New York, 1958.

PONTE, Lorenzo da: *Memoirs,* Dover Publications Inc., New York, 1967.

SADIE, Stanley: *Mozart,* Calder and Boyars Ltd., London.

SAINT-FOIX, G. de: *Les Symphonies de Mozart,* Editions Mellottée, Paris.

# Index of Names mentioned

*Printed by*
*IMPRIMERIE ELECTRA*
for
*HABITEX BOOKS*

### "SOCIAL" DISEASES

A Guide to the Recognition and Treatment of Venereal Disease

*Dr. Lionel Gendron*

—especially among the young. This book has been written so that the general reader may understand the causes, recognize the symptoms and appreciate the long-term effects of venereal disease.

*122 pages,*
*Fully illustrated*

### CELLULITE

*Dr. Gérard J. Léonard*

The author, one of the leading authorities on the subject in Canada, has written a book which will bring hope to all women who suffer from cellulite — hope founded on a scientifically based treatment which has been effective in reducing the problem.

*224 pages, Illustrated*

### WAITING FOR YOUR CHILD

*Yvette Pratte-Marchessault*

From the first signs of pregnancy to a complete course of postnatal exercises, this straightforward and informative new book provides the answers to the many questions a new mother may ask.

*192 pages, Fully illustrated with photographs and drawings*

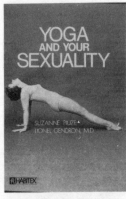

### YOGA AND YOUR SEXUALITY

*Suzanne Piuze and Lionel Gendron, M.D.*

Two well-known authors combine their special knowledge and skills to describe a particular kind of mental and physical harmony — that of mind and sexual function. Physical function is explained, along with the principles of yoga as they apply to a healthy mind and body.

*Fully illustrated*
*190 pages*

### VISUAL CHESS

*Henri Tranquille*

This book illustrates simple moves which occur in actual play and which are logical and easy to understand. Many celebrated attacks and defenses drawn from famous games are also included.

*175 pages, Illustrated in two colours*

### INTERPRETING YOUR DREAMS

*Louis Stanké*

This fascinating new book, in a dictionary format, will help the reader understand the significance of his dreams and appreciate the activity of his subconscious.

*176 pages*

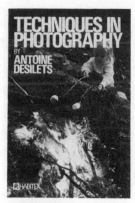

### TECHNIQUES IN PHOTOGRAPHY

*Antoine Desilets,*

An invaluable handbook for every one interested in photography — amateur and experienced alike.

*262 pages, Fully illustrated with photos, charts and diagrams*

### TAKING PHOTOGRAPHS

*Antoine Desilets in collaboration with Roland Weber*

A complete guide to taking photographs, covering such topics as Apparatus, Filters, Film, Light Meters, Flash Lighting, Viewpoint, Portraits and dozens of others.

*Fully illustrated 265 pages*

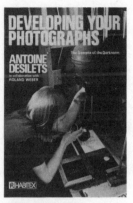

### DEVELOPING YOUR PHOTOGRAPHS

*Antoine Desilets in collaboration with Roland Weber*

Everything you need to know about developing your own films, from choosing basic equipment through enlarging to special effects. A question and answer technique deals with specific questions in detail.

*Fully illustrated, colour plates 335 pages*

### 8/SUPER 8/16

*André Lafrance*

Everything one might want to know about home movies, film making and film production is described in this handbook. It is intended primarily for the amateur, but is also an excellent reference for the more accomplished film-maker.

*Illustrated 245 pages*

### COMPLETE WOODSMAN

*Paul Provencher*

An invaluable handbook for the serious woodsman, this book is a basic guide to survival in the woods. It contains complete directions for every conceivable situation which might be encountered. A fascinating and useful handbook.

*Fully illustrated with line drawings — 225 pages*

### MUSIC IN QUEBEC 1600-1800

*Willy Amtmann*

The first survey of musical life in early Canada. It is not a history of music proper, concerning itself with the development of the art, but a cultural history stressing the musical aspects of the story of Canada's early years, of her difficulties, struggles and achievement.

## A GUIDE TO SELF-DEFENSE

*Louis Arpin*

This book is intended for men and women who are not necessarily sportsmen or athletes, but who want to know to defend themselves in an emergency.

*304 pages,*
*Fully illustrated*

## THE COMPLETE GUIDE TO JUDO

*Louis Arpin*

Beginning with the origins of the Martial Art known as the Way of Gentleness and proceeding through all the Ground and Standing techniques, this carefully written handbook will be invaluable to anyone interested in the sport.

*Fully illustrated*
*262 pages*

## SANKUKAI KARATE

*Me Yoshinao Nanbu*

Karate is a system of defense using no weapons — only feet, knees, elbows, fists, edges of the hands and fingertips. Sankukai karate is a form which uses many techniques developed by the author, Me Yoshinao Nanbu.

*Fully illustrated*
*235 pages*

## AIKIDO

*Text: M. N. di Villadorata*
*Photos: P. Grisard*

Until 1945 Aikido was "reserved" by the elite Japanese military establishment as its special form of self defense. It is a system of attack and defense where one or both participants are armed with staffs, spears, swords or knives.

*Fully illustrated*
*220 pages*

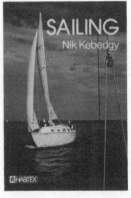

## SAILING

*Nik Kebedgy*

Not just a book for racers, *Sailing* describes some of the background of pleasure sailing and provides much valuable information about the more subtle aspects of the sport.

*Fully illustrated*
*275 pages*

## GARDENING

*Paul Pouliot*

Everything the amateur gardener might want to know about gardening in Canada is contained in this outstanding book by a leading Canadian agriculturalist. Topics range from preparing the soil through bulbs, grasses, trees, house plants and plant protection. A Gardening Calendar is a special feature.

*Illustrated*
*465 pages*

### LIVING IS SELLING

*Jean-Marc Chaput*

All the tricks of dynamic selling are revealed here by an experienced and successful salesman.

*198 pages*

### CARING FOR YOUR LAWN

*Paul Pouliot*

The complete guide to the development and maintenance of a beautiful lawn. The author provides many useful tips on lawn care.

*Fully illustrated*
*279 pages*

### HELP YOURSELF

*Psychotherapy Through Reason*

*Lucien Auger*
This guide to self-understanding provides a clear and simple method for overcoming emotional troubles.

*168 pages*

### MOZART SEEN THROUGH 50 MASTERPIECES

*Paul Roussel*

A fascinating account of Mozart's adult years and the circumstances surrounding the composition of 50 of his greatest works.

*344 pages*

### PHOTO GUIDE

*Antoine Desilets*

This simple guide provides a handy reference to the basics of still photography.

*Fully illustrated*
*45 pages*

### SUPER 8 CINE GUIDE

*André Lafrance*

A technical guide to super 8 photography, designed for use by the amateur as well as the professional.

*Fully illustrated*
*55 pages*

### A GUIDE TO HOME FREEZING

*Suzanne Lapointe*

This useful and comprehensive guide to the use of a home freezer is indispensable to anyone who plans ahead. Many ideas, recipes and suggestions are included.

*184 pages*

### A GUIDE TO HOME CANNING

*Sister Berthe*

An extensive collection of recipes for canning and preserving — ranging from meats and fish through to jams and jellies.

*264 pages*

### BLENDER RECIPES

*Juliette Huot*

A new collection of recipes and ideas for tasty and nutritious dishes which may be easily prepared using that most versatile kitchen tool — the blender.

*174 pages*

### FEEDING YOUR CHILD

*L. Lambert-Lagacé*

A useful and valuable guide to preparing nutritious meals for very young children.

*245 pages*